THE DOCTOR'S
PROTOCOL
FIELD
MANUAL

About Stansberry Research

Founded in 1999 and based out of Baltimore, Maryland, Stansberry Research is the largest independent source of financial insight in the world. It delivers unbiased investment advice to self-directed investors seeking an edge in a wide variety of sectors and market conditions.

Stansberry Research has nearly two dozen analysts and researchers – including former hedge-fund managers and buy-side financial experts. They produce a steady stream of timely research on value investing, income generation, resources, biotech, financials, short-selling, macroeconomic analysis, options trading, and more.

The company's unrelenting and uncompromised insight has made it one of the most respected and sought-after research organizations in the financial sector. It has nearly one million readers and more than 500,000 paid subscribers in over 100 countries.

About the Author

 Dr. Eifrig is the editor of three Stansberry Research newsletters... His largest monthly publication, *Retirement Millionaire,* shows 100,000-plus readers how to live a millionaire lifestyle on less money than you'd imagine possible. *Retirement Trader* shows readers a safe way to double or triple the gains in their retirement accounts with less risk. *Income Intelligence* shows investors how to analyze the income markets to maximize their income and total returns.

Doc has one of the best track records in the financial-newsletter business. From 2010 to 2014, he closed 136 winning positions in a row for his *Retirement Trader* subscribers.

Before joining Stansberry Research in 2008, Dr. Eifrig worked in arbitrage and trading groups with major Wall Street investment banks, including Goldman Sachs, Chase Manhattan, and Yamaichi in Japan. He has also published peer-reviewed medical research. After retiring from Wall Street, Dr. Eifrig attended medical school to become a board-eligible ophthalmologist. At Stansberry Research, he shares his love for empowering people with his finance and medical knowledge.

THE PROTOCOL

Please Note: all shortened web links in this field manual are case-specific.
For example, http://is.gd/6RbUpm is NOT the same as http://is.gd/6rbupm. If you are manually entering these links into your web browser's address bar, be sure to input the characters exactly as shown.

FOREWORD

Some days... I don't recognize the good ole U.S.A....

In 2013 government contractor Edward Snowden exposed the National Security Agency's top secret PRISM spying program. The 30-year-old whistleblower laid bare how aggressively the U.S. government now pries into the private lives of its citizens. PRISM is a warrantless domestic-surveillance nightmare. The program vacuums up and stores all American citizens' private e-mails, phone calls, web searches... everything.

He's taken residency in Russia. In a bid for his extradition, the U.S. government has promised the Russians it will not torture or execute Snowden.

Now, I don't know about you... but I remember when refugees from the then-Soviet Union fled to America from "the evil empire." They sought asylum from a totalitarian state able to torture or kill them... Today, the world is turned on its head.

Sadly, the existence of a domestic spying program like PRISM is outrageous... but hardly surprising.

Over the past dozen years, we've witnessed the growth of a massive police-state architecture in the United States. We have new internal security agencies (the Department of Homeland Security)... a monstrous internal travel security force (the Transportation Security Administration)... militarized local police departments... "peace officers" in black uniforms. They wield machine guns and even drive heavily armored vehicles in small towns like Franklin, Indiana.

The government has created all of this in the name of "fighting terror-ism." And in the wake of the horrific terrorist attacks of September 11, 2001... many folks might say the threat of another attack justifies the government's actions. But here's an interesting statistic I've never seen reported in any major media outlet...

> The U.S. National Counter Terrorism Center released its 2011 annual report last year. Of the 13,288 people killed by terrorist attacks worldwide, just seventeen (17) were private U.S. citizens, or 0.001%.

That means out of a total U.S. population of 315 million, terrorists killed 0.0000053968254% of us. By way of comparison, Americans are as likely to die from a terrorist attack as they are from household appliances falling on them. These are the statistics.

As a medical doctor and former Wall Street trader, I've focused my entire professional life on sound analysis of facts and statistics. I prefer to leave the realm of hype and conjecture to others. Today, the U.S. police state is perhaps the worst example of the damage irrational, fear-driven deci-sions can cause.

Similar decisions in our individual lives – especially when made during crisis situations – have the potential to destroy our fortunes, our families, our futures. Helping people avoid these critical mistakes was the inspira-tion behind this book.

This field manual is designed to help you insure against the most likely dangers out there. Its scientific approach boils everything down to what I really care about – facts. From these facts, I've developed a protocol that – when fully implemented – will provide you a level of confidence and security most can only dream about. You'll never let irrational fears dominate your decision-making processes again. This could save your life.

Whether you are exiting a burning building... enduring an extended power outage... escaping a crashed jet-liner... shipping your assets offshore... or overcoming any number of possible adversities, this book will empower you to take the actions necessary to safeguard the wellbeing of yourself and your family.

That's "sleep at night" confidence you can't put a price on. And it's what I hope to impart to you by the end of this book.

Here's to our health, wealth, and a great retirement,

Dr. David Eifrig Jr. MD, MBA
Editor, *Retirement Millionaire*
November 2014

P.S. A special thanks to Josh Reeves who assisted diligently in the creation of this book.

STEP ONE
✚ PREPARE

Rick Rescorla may be the greatest American hero you've never heard of...

A decorated Vietnam veteran of British birth, Rescorla was the head of security for Morgan Stanley's World Trade Center offices in New York City. With a workforce of nearly 3,000 people, the bank was the towers' largest tenant.

Although Rescorla's heroics hold a special place in the hearts of Morgan Stanley employees, his deep understanding of crises made him a pain in the neck some days...

Rescorla was an expert disaster planner. He worried that the World Trade Center represented a major terrorist target. So he put Morgan Stanley employees through frequent, random evacuation drills.

When Rescorla's evacuation drill orders came, everything stopped. Every last person was taught the evacuation routes, time limits, and contingency plans... and everyone would practice them. Although Morgan Stanley traded hundreds of millions of dollars a day through its World Trade Center offices, employees had to participate in Rescorla's evacuation drills.

Rescorla appointed team leaders and fire marshals for every floor. They underwent extra training. Their jobs were to make sure the different floors would follow his comprehensive 22-floor evacuation plan. Every visitor to Morgan Stanley would receive a proper safety briefing before conducting any business in the offices.

Some folks found Rescorla's drills annoying. They wanted to skip the interruptions and keep working.

On September 11, 2001, the first plane hit Tower 1 at 8:46 a.m. The Morgan Stanley offices were in Tower 2. Office workers felt the explosion

1

and saw the damage. They could see people breaking out windows and crawling out to escape the heat and flames. Some were jumping.

Shortly after impact, the Port Authority came across the buildings' intercom system. The order was for everyone, in both towers, to stay put... But Rescorla was already out taking action... right according to plan.

He ordered his security staff, floor leaders, and fire marshals to evacuate immediately. He picked up his walkie-talkie and bullhorn and commanded the operation, floor by floor. The Morgan Stanley evacuation plan went into full effect... and the people responded the moment the order came down. They had been drilled in exactly what to do.

Seventeen minutes later, at 9:03 a.m., the second plane hit Tower 2. The jolt knocked people off their feet. Desks and file cabinets overturned. Papers littered the floors. The power went out. Many sustained injuries in the stairwells and on the Morgan Stanley floors. The stress on everyone jumped from high to extreme. But the evacuation continued according to plan.

Rescorla knew everyone in the building was in serious trouble now. His people were performing well, but he needed to maintain their focus. He didn't want anyone freezing... so he picked up his bullhorn and began singing songs from his youth. They were the same songs he'd sung to his men back in Vietnam. They helped people keep fear at bay and focus on the task at hand. The songs worked just as well in the World Trade Center stairwells as they did during the war.

In between songs, Rescorla paused to call his wife. "Stop crying," he told her, "I have to get these people out safely. If something should happen to me, I want you to know I've never been happier. You made my life."

By around 9:45, the evacuation of Morgan Stanley's offices was nearly complete. But at the bottom, Rescorla turned around and started heading back up. A handful of people were unaccounted for, plus members of his security staff.

Then, there were the firemen, police, and people from every other office in the building. Everyone knew Rescorla wouldn't come out until every last person had been rescued.

Rick Rescorla, American hero, was last seen in the 10th floor stairwell, heading higher. Not long after that, at 9:59 a.m., Tower 2 collapsed.

Just thirteen Morgan Stanley employees died on 9/11. This includes Rescorla and four of his security team. But the remaining 2,687 employees, plus 250 office visitors, survived.

They survived in large part thanks to Rescorla and his knowledge of something called "negative panic."

They survived because Rick Rescorla had a plan.

The Biggest Misconception About Disasters

When I say the word "disaster," what comes to mind?

If you're like most people, you immediately think about panicked crowds and mass hysteria. You probably envision riots, chaos, and people rushing about, trying to save themselves.

But guess what...

Scientists have studied the crisis phenomenon over and over again. It turns out this is NOT what happens.

In fact, the most common reaction to any crisis is the complete opposite of what I just described. Contrary to popular belief, most people don't freak out.

They simply freeze.

Researchers refer to this response as "negative panic."

It's an involuntary, and often very dangerous, response. It's what happens to most people... despite what you see on television and in the movies.

In a real-world crisis, people lose all ability to make rational decisions. They become statues and do little – or nothing – to escape a life-threatening situation.

That's why disaster plans and drills created by people like Rick Rescorla are so important. They train people to fight "negative panic" and react in a way that saves lives.

You may say to yourself, "The World Trade Center example is extreme. Nothing like that will ever happen to me."

I hope you're right. I hope nothing "extreme" happens to you.

If you're part of the tiny percentage of Americans who NEVER experience a real crisis in your life, consider yourself one of the very lucky ones.

But realize that every day, regular Americans just like you and me are faced with floods, tornadoes, deranged murderers, hurricanes, stock market crashes, rapists, and dozens other crisis-causing events and people. And plenty of crises occur in ways that don't make headlines. Health emergencies, home fires, and household accidents all can elicit "negative panic" with dangerous or fatal consequences.

In just the past 15 years, Americans have dealt with the 9/11 attacks... Hurricane Katrina... the 2008 financial crisis... the shootings in Columbine, Newtown, and Aurora... and the Boston Marathon bombing, just to name a few.

As I mentioned, I hope you never have to deal with a serious disaster. But over a lifetime, it's very likely that you will.

That's why I've put together this special emergency-preparedness manual.

In it, you'll find techniques, plans, and strategies to help you handle the kinds of disasters we regularly face as Americans.

Before we get into the dangers we all face and how to effectively deal with them, let me get back to one of the biggest misconceptions of dealing with crisis.

As I mentioned, the most common reaction to a crisis situation is not chaos... but rather what's called "negative panic."

My Lesson From Wall Street

I became a physician for my second career. Prior to that I earned my MBA and began my professional life on Wall Street. I've worked at the trading desks of some of the most powerful banking institutions in the world, including Goldman Sachs.

The interesting thing is... I saw the "negative panic" response as much in the financial markets as I did in my medical studies.

Trading the financial markets is not for the undisciplined. Billions of dollars are transferred between parties every day. Traders employ a wide variety of techniques to try to predict what the market will do. But most of these are rational approaches... Yet, the irrationality of human beings leads to outcomes that are less than logical.

I've seen individuals with huge open trades freeze up when the market turned against them. The stress and fear in the moment overwhelmed them. They had no backup plan in place. They didn't know how to respond. And they rode their losing trades all the way to the bottom.

It's ugly. It's sad to say, but I've even known of traders who took their own lives after such trades went awry.

That's why one of the first lessons I learned on Wall Street was this simple mantra:

"Plan the Trade, Then Trade the Plan"

Plan the Trade... This means you make all your preparations ahead of time, including – and this is critical – contingency plans for when things go wrong. You always have at least one exit strategy BEFORE entering a trade. Multiple exit strategies are better. This way you will know how to react in a stressful environment.

Trade the Plan... This means you execute your plan to the letter. It may seem like an easy thing to do. The truth is, powerful emotions well up inside you in stressful circumstances. Focusing your attention on following your plan often means the difference between success and failure.

My friends in the military have told me a similar phrase. They call it the "8 Ps":

"Proper Prior Planning and Preparation Prevents Piss-Poor Performance"

That's why in war movies we always hear the veterans tell their new comrades, "Remember your training." The military has a checklist or flowchart for just about every possible procedure. It might seem to go a bit overboard sometimes... but in crises, the training and preparation can make the difference in whether people live or die.

Whether you follow the "8 Ps" or my own personal trading mantra, the point is you must be prepared to act ahead of time.

Waiting for the crisis to unfold is too late. Our brains shut down under extreme fear. You'll have no hope of trying to reason out what to do, when minutes (or even seconds) mean the difference between life and death.

The benefits of having a prior plan – or protocol, as I call it – are twofold. First, the protocol is a roadmap for how to navigate out of a crisis. Knowing what to do is a tremendous benefit to you and your family.

Second, *knowing that you know what to do is* an even more powerful benefit. This knowledge alone builds confidence and reduces fear. If fear doesn't spike to extreme levels inside you, you'll be unlikely to ever succumb to negative panic. Your confidence will allow you to take appropriate action while fear paralyzes others.

In 1646, Jesuit priest Athanasius Kircher noted a curious condition in animals under duress.

When gripped in the hands of a human attacker, some wild creatures would squawk, flail, and struggle for five to 10 seconds. Then... the animals would go catatonic. Their temperature dropped. Their respiration increased. Their heart rates slowed. Their eyes stayed open, but their gazes were unfocused. The animals became calm and quiet in the face of certain death. They could stay in this trance-like state for 20 minutes or more.

Kirchner was able to "bewitch" blackbirds, eagles, peacocks, and owls in this way. His work was the earliest academic record of what some have called "animal hypnosis." And birds are not the only animals to exhibit these tendencies.

Recent experiments have shown frogs, crabs, lobsters, lizards, snakes, boars, cows, rabbits, and primates — including humans — all exhibit the same hypnotic reaction when faced with imminent doom. In humans, psychologists have called this reaction "negative panic."

It turns out this "hypnosis" is an evolutionary survival tactic. By playing dead, the prey signals to the predator that it may be rotten or diseased. It's a ruse designed to play to the predator's own evolutionary survival instincts: The best way to keep living is to avoid ingesting poison.

Modern experiments seem to indicate two necessary conditions for negative panic to strike humans. First, people must feel trapped. Second, they must feel extreme fear.

The good news is that we can prevent ourselves from ever succumbing to animal hypnosis or negative panic. There are proven ways to control these feelings. The critical factor is... we must prepare ahead of time. We must have a plan in place, and we must practice it. Trying to handle the overpowering grip of fear in the midst of a crisis is too late.

The chapters that follow will provide the foundation for this confidence. Specifically, I'm talking about the four steps in what I call my Doctor's Protocol.

These steps are:

No. 1: PREPARE

No. 2: PROVISION

No. 3: PROTECT

No. 4: PROSPER

Once you learn these simple techniques, you will be prepared for just about anything nature or mankind can throw at you. I believe it will give you a whole new outlook on life, too.

Crises and the occasional disaster are just a part of life. You have to accept that fact. And when you are prepared, these things become merely nuisances, rather than life-changing events.

I personally know that no matter what happens, I can deal with it. So I don't lose a minute of sleep thinking about these types of problems.

My Doctor's Protocol will give you just about everything you need to know. I've read the books. I've studied the science. And I've boiled it all down to just the information you really need to know.

Last, I've taken my research and included one final bonus chapter called "Secrets of Survival." The contents inside will help you synthesize the four steps of my protocol. They will let you take immediate action to protect yourself and prosper. You will have no trouble handling adversity in a way you never thought possible.

Let's get started.

PREPARE: Step No. 1 of The Doctor's Protocol

The first step in my Doctor's Protocol is called PREPARE.

What does this mean exactly?

Well... this is the most-often overlooked part of nearly every preparedness plan. Most people tend to focus exclusively on what they "have." But in reality, supplies are much less important than PREPARE.

By PREPARE, we mean several things:

1. To gain an understanding of what really happens in a crisis.

2. To understand how you and your family are likely to react in a crisis situation, and...

3. To know exactly what steps you must take. To have a plan.

PREPARE helps you understand how a crisis really unfolds and how groups and individuals react to stressful situations... then implement a strong strategic plan.

When I explain this critical step to people, the usual reaction that I get is that it sounds "simple"... and some even dismiss it as "common sense."

But remember... you will not respond to a crisis situation the way you behave in normal life. In a true crisis situation, your brain basically shuts down.

For example, paramedics say it's common for people dealing with a loved one's emergency to get a neighbor to dial 911 for them because they just can't perform such a seemingly simple operation.

Think about that for a minute... The rush of chemicals coupled with the complete unfamiliarity with the situation makes it almost impossible for many people to pick up the phone and hit three numbers.

The good news is, you have several ways to fight this.

Know Thyself

Remember... negative panic is an evolutionary, involuntary coping mechanism that feigns death. It strikes people who feel terrified and trapped.

In caveman days, playing dead to make a saber-toothed tiger lose interest in you might have been a good survival tactic. But in a fire, flood, crash, or other similar disaster, negative panic leads to near-certain death. That's why in our modern world, we must avoid slipping into this state of mind.

To do this, we need to look into human psychology...

Disaster researchers have determined humans typically go through three mental stages in a crisis. Remember these. Being able to recognize what stage you're in is one way you'll keep from slipping into negative panic.

We'll call these stages the "Three Ds":

1. **Stage 1 - Disbelief**

2. **Stage 2 - Deliberation**

3. **Stage 3 - Decisiveness**

This order is the usual progression of stages. Remember, there are no absolutes... Both the order and the amount of time spent in each stage varies. The important thing to remember is... you want to get yourself into Stage 3 as fast as possible. Stage 3 is the only stage where you can take the decisive actions to save your life.

Let's look at each stage a bit closer.

Stage 1 – Disbelief:

The brain works by taking experiential data and comparing it with models it has already formed to understand the world. Most of our everyday lives fit into one of these models. Unless you have a "first responder" type of job, emergencies are not a regular occurrence.

When an emergency happens, the data our brains receive won't mesh with our normal models. So it tries to shoehorn the situation into a familiar model. It does this through reacting in denial or disbelief.

A great example of disbelief occurred in the Morgan Stanley offices on 9/11. Rick Rescorla made every effort to prepare his coworkers for an emergency. But after the first plane hit, one senior vice president stayed at his desk. He kept conducting business on the phone. He refused to evacuate with the rest of his floor.

He was in complete disbelief. He denied that he was in any danger... and he paid for his disbelief with his life. Tragically, he was also one of the reasons Rescorla went back up into the burning tower after he'd rescued almost everyone else.

When something happens outside your normal experience, you must recognize it as such. Don't say to yourself "oh, it'll be OK" or "the authorities will tell me if I should worry about this." You need to recognize you're in danger. The sooner you do this, the sooner you move past Stage 1.

Stage 2 – Deliberation:

A person moves past Stage 1 when he accepts the reality of the situation. Now, he must do something about it. But what? This is the start of Stage 2, deliberation.

Some people have a hard time deciding what they will eat for dinner. They can run internal deliberations for hours. Imagine trying to deliberate the best way to save your life... right in the middle of a terrifying ordeal. It's difficult, dangerous, and deadly.

We may wonder what went through the mind of the Morgan Stanley executive who stayed behind and kept working. After the second plane hit Tower 2 (his own building), do you think he started to deliberate how to escape?

Would he go down towards the ground? Would he go up towards the roof? Would he have to jump, like he saw people doing from Tower 1? I'm sure he felt trapped and terrified... Odds are good he succumbed to negative panic and simply froze.

The point is you do NOT want to spend too much time deliberating in a crisis. You want to know exactly what to do ahead of time. If you already have a contingency plan, there is little need for deliberation. You just execute the plan. Just like my lesson from trading on Wall Street.

Which brings us to...

Stage 3 – Decisiveness:

This is the moment you take action. You start to carry out the plan in place. This should be a pre-determined, well-reasoned, and rehearsed plan.

Rescorla's prior evacuation instruction and drilling put almost every Morgan Stanley employee into "instant Stage 3" when the actual crisis struck. His fire marshals and floor leaders began taking action even before his actual evacuation order.

Thousands of people survived because of this instant "fast-forward" to Stage 3 – decisiveness.

To be able to do this in our own lives, we must...

Learn and practice this vital anti-fear tactic.

Before you ever begin making your disaster response plans, I have a powerful technique you can implement right away. It's something every American should know to avoid falling into negative panic... even if you don't yet have a ready response plan.

It's a simple exercise used by the Green Berets, FBI agents, and police officers around the country. It's called "Combat Breathing" in some circles... and "Tactical Breathing" in others.

I'll teach you how to do it right now... in less than one minute.

Here's how it works...

Breathing is one of the few actions that can be controlled by both our somatic nervous system (the things we can consciously control, like moving your arm or sticking out your tongue) and our autonomic nervous system (which includes things we can't typically voluntarily control, like heart rate, perspiration, and digestion).

You breathe automatically, without thinking about it... but you can also consciously change the way you breathe, at least for a brief period of time.

Breathing is a bridge – for most people, the only bridge – between these two nervous systems. By controlling it, you can alter the way your entire body responds in a crisis.

If you find yourself freezing up... starting to panic... or if you are having a hard time figuring out exactly what to do next in any crisis situation, the first thing you should do is try this simple four-step "Combat Breathing" technique.

Combat Breathing Technique

Step 1. **Breathe in for a count of four.**

Step 2. **Hold your breath for a count for four.**

Step 3. **Exhale for a count of four.**

Step 4. **Count to four before starting over again.**

That's it.

I know, it sounds incredibly simple, but the next time you feel stressed... or even the slightest bit panicked, give it a shot for just a minute or two. I guarantee it will change the way your body is responding. It will calm you down... help you think much more clearly... and help you take action.

Make Combat Breathing the universal first step of every crisis response plan right now.

The breathing technique I described can help you right away... even if you don't have your crisis response plans ready. That's why I've listed it first.

But combat breathing should be a way to enhance your response plan... not your only emergency skill.

The next step to avoid negative panic is to get familiar with your own natural crisis response.

Take stock of your life and your circumstances.

The ideas above should give you a better sense of your internal crisis response. This basic awareness may seem simplistic, but it is vital. It will help you break through to Stage 3: Decisiveness.

Let's begin fleshing out what the rest of your response plans will look like. All good plans have two fundamental components - a strategic goal and tactics to achieve this goal.

Said another way, your strategy defines what you are trying to accomplish. Your tactics determine how you will accomplish it.

Let's begin to devise some emergency-response strategies. We will base these on the given realities of your circumstances.

I'd like for you to think about the situations in your life that would leave you vulnerable. For example, what would you do if...

- Your house is broken into.
- The power goes out for days or weeks.
- You lose your job.
- You're held up by an armed assailant.
- You endure a natural disaster.
- You get drawn into a physical altercation.
- The modern communications grid goes down.
- You're told to evacuate your hometown.
- You're caught in a terrorist attack.
- Your home catches fire.
- You're involved in a transportation accident.

Everyone's circumstances are unique. Everyone's response plan will be different. There are no "one size fits all" answers to these questions. The important thing is to reflect on scenarios like the ones above.

So right now go back and read each line while practicing Combat Breathing.

Your goal will be to come out of these emergencies in one piece. Try to think of other crises that apply to your unique circumstances.

Of course, you can go overboard with this phase. You cannot – and should not – try to prepare for everything. But what you can do is prepare for the crises that are most likely... and those that are potentially catastrophic for you and your family.

In my bonus chapter, "Secrets to Survival," I'll give you some specific guidelines for responses to threats like these. But I'm not going to list those here...

For now, just take note of potential disaster situations, and start to conceive of how you will respond to them. Doing this mental "legwork" now will calm and empower you when the crisis occurs. Remember, the PREPARE stage is about preparing your most important crisis response tool... your mind.

You may want to write these ideas down. You'll refer to them as you progress through the protocol.

Use this manual to help round out general threat awareness.

Acute crises are always the things that grip the imagination. People always wonder how they would react in a plane crash or terrorist incident.

My protocol will give you some important tips should you ever find yourself caught in one of these situations. But the reality is, the chances of these dramatic misfortunes striking you are slim.

In 2012, the National Counter Terrorism Center released a report on terrorism-related deaths. It concluded Americans are as likely to die from a terrorist attack as they are from household appliances falling on them. These are the statistical facts.

14

The crises most Americans are likely to face seem more mundane... but are no less threatening to your survival. Health emergencies, house fires, and accidents are far more common and require at least as much preparation.

Regular *Retirement Millionaire* readers know I focus my analysis on facts and statistics... and leave the realm of hype and conjecture to others. The facts say that fire is the disaster that kills more Americans every year than all other disasters combined.

This protocol is all about helping you provide insurance against the most likely dangers out there. Fire is a universal threat... but others are more location-specific.

I've found a free online resource that can help acquaint you with the disasters you are most likely to face. It provides you tailored response suggestions based upon your location.

You can check it out at this website:
http://www.ready.gov/today

Please note: The Federal Emergency Management Agency (FEMA) maintains this website. I cannot endorse all of its prescribed solutions. We've all witnessed the government mishandle too many crises to trust it to do the right thing. But I do like this website's state-by-state resource page. At a minimum, it will help open your eyes to some of the most likely threats to you and your family.

Learn the skills needed to exit the crisis.

The steps above have helped you center your mind. They're also assisting you in devising a comprehensive preparedness strategy.

Plan the Trade, Trade the Plan

In our mantra, they're all designed to help you "**plan the trade**." But that is only half the battle...

In order to master the other half – to "**trade the plan**" – you must have the appropriate skill sets necessary to put your plans into motion.

The information that follows is some of the most valuable in my whole PREPARE protocol. There is a way to get free, professional-grade disaster-response training. I've uncovered a program that will bring your skills up in a hurry.

It's called the Community Emergency Response Team (CERT). It's funded through FEMA. But it's administered by local emergency responders, like your neighborhood fire department.

The government established the program to bring regular citizens into the formal disaster-response process. CERT members receive training on how to handle a wide range of crises. This includes everything from natural disasters to biological attacks to basic medical emergencies.

CERT classes also teach you the inner workings of government readiness plans. Upon graduation, you will be credentialed. The program will even outfit you with uniform items and equipment. All of this may afford you greater access and mobility in times of emergency. If the government sets up checkpoints or relief camps, a CERT credential could make it easier for you to navigate through the system.

Practice, practice, practice.

This is the final component of the PREPARE protocol. It's also the most important of all. The previous ideas helped you add new tools to your emergency-response "toolkit." These provide the framework for staying calm and focused in a crisis. Use them to avoid falling into negative panic.

But even the sharpest blade dulls over time. It is not enough to have an academic understanding of how to act. You must practice these skills if they are to remain with you.

Remember, the last thing you want to do is try to think through a crisis. Practice is the only way you will learn to move quickly through the stages and take immediate action. The vital information in my entire Doctor's Protocol is useless unless you practice it. That's why this is the most important component of all.

Think back to when you were first learning to drive. You had to think through how to change lanes or make a left-hand turn. Now, you don't

When to Trust the Government

To be clear, I make a distinction between the government's emergency-response strategies vs. its emergency-response tactics. CERT training will teach you both, but I believe the tactical side holds the greatest direct benefit. This includes acute life-saving skills.

Learning how the government plans to respond is also beneficial, but mostly so you can know how to work around and through its inefficient plans.

Make no mistake, I am not just "government bashing." The following is a direct quote from a government CERT instructor. Author Neil Strauss took the course in Los Angeles. He chronicled his experiences in the book, *Emergency: This Book Will Save Your Life.*

"'You cannot count on us... Nobody's coming to your aid in a disaster,' [Kevin Mason, Strauss' CERT instructor] said. [The CERT class] had already taught me that my expectation that the government would save and protect its citizens after Hurricane Katrina was unreasonable.

"According to Mason, the federal plan was and always had been: let the mess happen and hope the people take care of themselves. Then come in, scoop up the survivors, and help the community recover."

You see... we're on our own. Emergency readiness is everyone's individual responsibility. But we can gain superior response skills through programs like CERT. Knowing that you know what to do (and how to do it) breeds confidence. I can't promise you'll never succumb to negative panic... but for a well-trained individual with a plan, the chances are greatly reduced.

even think about it... you just do it. The car feels like an extension of your body. How did you master this skill?

Practice.

The Doctor's Protocol Step No. 1: PREPARE

STEP TWO
⚡🏠 PROVISION

The first of our four-step Doctor's Protocol – PREPARE – covers the most important aspect of any readiness plan... preparing the mind for crisis. Step No. 2 covers PROVISION. While the first step helps with the mental aspects of crises, the second step teaches you about the physical things you might need. Let's start by discussing what sorts of crises you could face. That will help identify the things you'll need.

Know Thyself, Know Thy Crisis

Crises come in two main varieties – acute and enduring.

As I mentioned in Step No. 1, acute crises tend to be the ones that stick out in people's minds. A man who wakes up in a house engulfed in flames is in the middle of an acute crisis. He must take immediate action to survive.

I give specific details about how to survive several acute crises in the bonus chapter, "Secrets of Survival." But these are not the types of emergencies that require action ahead of time... enduring crises are.

Enduring crises don't normally captivate the imagination... But they are the ones you are most likely to experience. Enduring crises may begin as acute crises – like an earthquake or hurricane – but they end up lasting far beyond the initial shock.

Consider this "enduring" example...

In Step No. 2: PROVISION, I'll also share with you how much of these items you'll need. In general, I recommend one week of reserves as the minimum amount to keep on hand. Or can increase/decrease your reserves in accordance with how long you feel you might be "off the grid."

No matter what you decide, I encourage you to stick to the adage: "Better safe than sorry." If you can afford it, your level of preparation should exceed your level of risk.

It's Never a Question of "if"...

On a hot summer afternoon on August 14, 2003, two power lines in Walton Hills, Ohio sagged down into a nearby tree.

Power lines sag when they are overloaded. The extra electricity coursing through the lines heats them up. This causes them to expand and sag. And on this summer day, everyone in town was running his air conditioner... drawing a ton of power through those overloaded lines.

When two sagging lines touched nearby trees, the contact tripped the local power station's safety override mechanism. The system shut off power to the lines. The shutdown forced other lines to carry a higher load... which in turn caused them to sag into other nearby trees. The process repeated again and again.

By 3:17 p.m., the local Ohio power station was producing more electricity than it could distribute through available lines. Emergency systems took the plant offline to prevent generator overload. Other plants increased output to compensate. But similar faults in antiquated power lines and emergency shutoff systems forced these plants to shut down as well. A cascade reaction began.

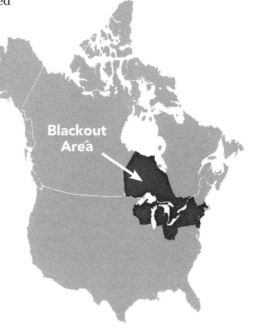

By 4:13 p.m., 256 power plants across eight northeast states and one Canadian province had gone offline. Fifty-five million people were left without power... for days.

As day wore into night, chaos began to unfold. Burglar alarms were inoperable, so break-ins and lootings spiked. Waves of panicked emergency calls overwhelmed police, fire departments, and emergency medical responders. In New York City, emergency services responded to more than 80,000 calls for help, more than twice the usual amount.

In Michigan, one man ran a gas generator inside his home and died from carbon-monoxide inhalation. Another died after falling asleep with candles lit... The fire spread to nearby curtains and engulfed his home in flames. Four million citizens across the state were under a boil-water advisory for days.

Stress-induced heart attacks killed medicine-deprived elderly citizens. Reckless motorists killed children riding bikes through unlit streets.

In city after darkened city, those without cash on hand had no way to purchase vital goods... nor could they withdraw funds from banks or ATMs. Commerce ground to a near standstill as the entire populace waited and wondered... "What do we do now?"

The northeast blackout of 2003 was the second-largest in world history, at the time. It contributed to at least 11 fatalities. For most involved, it was a dangerous and uncomfortable time. In the worst cases, the outage proved lethal.

Recently, U.S. citizens were reminded of how awful these situations are when "Superstorm" Sandy struck the Eastern Seaboard in the summer of 2012. Residents of New York City and New Jersey went days without power.

Unexpected, disruptive events are a fact of life. It is never a question of "if"... it is only a matter of "when." There's no good reason to be at the mercy of these unexpected, but inevitable, events. You can take some simple steps right now to protect you and your family against enduring crises like the 2003 power outage.

My Doctor's Protocol Step No. 2: PROVISION is about determining the basic supplies you need to become more self-reliant. It's a critical part of your readiness.

Must-Have Items for Surviving an Enduring Crisis

1. Water
2. Food
3. Power
4. Communications
5. Emergency Contacts
6. Money

1. Water. Water tops the list because it is most critical to your survivability. The human body can last for weeks without food, but only a few days without water.

You should keep at least one gallon of water per person per day in reserve for drinking purposes. If you live in an arid climate, you may want to store up to three gallons of water per person per day. Use the formula below to calculate the total amount of water you need.

How to Calculate Water Needed

_____ x _____ x _____ = _____
(No. of people) (No. of gallons) (No. of days)   (Total gallons needed)

So if you have four people in your family... and plan for one gallon of drinking water per day for each person... and you plan to keep a seven-day supply... you'll need to store at least 28 gallons of water (4 x 1 x 7 = 28).

*** Five-gallon "water cooler" jugs may be the easiest and most economical way to stock up. One-gallon jugs may fit better into available shelving.

Using the example from above, 6 five-gallon jugs of water would give you 30 gallons, meeting your minimum needs with two extra gallons to spare.

*** Please Note: It's fine to store water in your garage. **But don't put plastic containers directly on cement floors.**

Most people don't realize **storing plastic water bottles on concrete can start a chemical reaction and contaminate the water.** To be safe, store them on plywood or another nonporous membrane.

***Original, unopened water containers are best for long-term storage. While they may have six-month "best before" dates, water does not "go bad." The issue to be aware of is contamination. Water containers that you have refilled yourself are more apt to contain microbes.

If you choose to fill your own water jugs, sanitize them first. Use a ratio of one teaspoon of bleach to one gallon of water. Shake the bleached gallon of water in one container for 10 seconds and let sit for a minute; repeat about three times. Rinse with drinking water and let dry before filling with the water you intend to store.

Be careful not to contaminate the inside of the lid with your hands. Rinse the lids with the bleach-and-water mixture before putting it back on the bottles.

*** With both water and food storage, *the best practice is to rotate the stored items into your regular consumption patterns.* Even though water lasts longer than six months, it would be best to consume the stored water and restock, twice per year.

*** If you know a crisis may be coming (like an approaching hurricane), do what I do and fill up every tub or basin you have with water *before* the storm hits. Leave one sink empty for washing and drainage.

The average bathtub can hold about 60 gallons. Don't forget about laundry-room sinks and tubs. (They're usually quite deep.) I even start my washing machine and then turn it off once the basin fills. This adds another 10-20 gallons of ready water.

The water that fills these basins is the same water that comes out of your kitchen tap. *As long as the basins are clean,* this water is safe to drink. But I prefer to save the washing-machine water for washing and sanitation.

*** If you've exhausted your supply of stored drinking water and still need more, you've got options. Most people forget that their hot water heaters are water reserves.

The average water heater contains about 40 gallons of water. It's the same water that comes out of your kitchen faucet. Attach a garden hose to the bottom release valve to tap into this emergency water backup.

*** Tap water collected after a power outage occurs may not be safe to drink. Drinking contaminated water can make you *very* ill, very quickly.

Use the following techniques to stay safe:

- Boil Water: Bringing water to a boil for three minutes will make it safe to drink (after it cools). But don't let it boil for more than three minutes. After that, valuable clean water starts to evaporate.
- Sterilization: Add two to four drops of chlorine bleach per quart of water. Let it sit for 30 minutes. Smell the water. It should smell like chlorine. If it doesn't, repeat the process. Wait another 30 minutes before drinking.
- Solar Water Disinfection: If you cannot do either of the methods above, you can utilize the sun's ultraviolet radiation to make water safe to drink. CAUTION: You must follow these exact instructions. Failure to do so will result in unsafe drinking water!

    » Use CLEAR, PLASTIC containers no larger than two liters

    » Remove exterior labels

    » Fill with clear, particle-filtered water (cannot be murky)

    » Expose bottled water to direct sunlight for six hours.

This method works as long as the container is made of plastic (not glass), is clear (not blue or some other color), and is low volume. (Ultraviolet radiation cannot penetrate dense concentrations of water.)

For more detailed info on why and how solar water disinfection (so-called "sodis") works, visit: http://www.sodis.ch/index_EN.

*** So far, we've only discussed potable or "drinking" water. Don't forget, water is important for washing and sanitation as well. You can reuse cooking water for other purposes. I'll cover these issues in detail in Step No. 3 of my Doctor's Protocol - PROTECT.

2. Food. Just as with water, you will want to keep at least one week of food per person in reserve. The best foods to buy for storage purposes are staples in your regular diet. Then, *you can rotate them into your regular consumption patterns* before their expiration dates approach.

Canned vegetables, beans, and soup work best for this. You can also store canned meats and fish, like chicken, tuna, and salmon.

Canned food may "keep" for longer than one year... but its nutritional value breaks down faster than its palatability. As a result, you'll need to eat more just to feel "full"... and this could end up turning what you thought was two weeks of food into less than you expected.

Bottom line: It's important to keep canned foods "fresh." Rotate them into your normal consumption. At most, keep canned food for no longer than one year. If you find cans in your stockpile bulging at the ends, the food inside has spoiled. Throw them out. Never eat a can that looks like it's about to burst, no matter how hungry you are. Remember this adage, "When in doubt, throw it out."

*** When the power goes out, eat your most perishable food first. This means the stuff in the refrigerator. Try not to open the door until you know what you need and close it again as fast as possible. Refrigerated food can last about six hours. Frozen food will thaw out by the second day. Again, keep the freezer door shut as long as possible.

Only after perishable food (refridgerated food first then frozen) is gone should you dip into canned goods... and finally emergency supplies.

*** Something most Americans don't understand is a simple rule of thermodynamics when keeping food cold...

When the power docs go out, throwing blankcts on top and around the refrigerator/freezer will extend the time the interior stays cool. Just be sure not to cover the backside or any vents you see (usually at the bottom). Covering these areas when the power comes back on will reduce efficiency and could become a fire hazard.

*** Did you know that a full freezer will keep food cold for twice as long as a half-full freezer? You don't want to have a lot of "dead air" inside the freezer. If you know a big storm is coming, with the potential for long **power outages, pack your freezer as full as you can get it.**

Even in regular times, do what I do... Load up the unused space in your freezer with bottled water. This will help keep the food cold longer when the power goes out. It will also give you an extra reserve of drinking water when it melts.

This tactic also helps lower your utility bills and extend freezer life. Just be sure to leave room in the bottles for the water to expand. Water expands by about 10% when it freezes.

*** Dried items like rice, beans, and dehydrated potatoes also keep for long periods without spoiling. Powdered drink additives (like Gatorade, Tang, etc.) last even longer and can add variety to your drink choices.

*** **The absolute best food for emergency prep is canned soup.** It's the main surplus food supply I keep in my own home. It's compact and easy to store. It will give you all the nutrients you need. And it keeps for a long time.

There's also one other cheap, "secret" survival food that beats all the rest. In terms of cost per calorie, **you can't do better than old fashioned peanut butter.** Peanut butter is a compact way to provide protein, dietary fiber, some carbs, and fat. It also stores well. Try to buy whole peanut butter. The ingredients should include nothing more than peanuts and salt. Of course, if you must get the popular sugary peanut butter for your family's taste... I understand.

Also in terms of longevity, the "fantastic four" – whole wheat, honey, salt, and powdered nonfat milk (a great source of protein) – will keep almost indefinitely. If your emergency lasts longer than you have canned food in reserve, these foods provide another layer of safety. (Of course, to use whole wheat, you need to learn how to mill it.)

*** Long-term, hermetically sealed (i.e., airtight) storable food products are another option. Several companies offer packaged foods designed to be stored for up to 20 years. The danger with these is that they may or may not live up to their promises. This would be unfortunate to discover in a crisis, when you need the food the most. The rotation approach to food storage ensures you have reliable reserves.

If you want to buy this type of product as an emergency backup, I recommend you shop at Costco. I cannot personally vouch for the longevity of the products (give me about 18 more years). But the company's track record of providing high-quality products at great prices makes me comfortable buying them. Do what I do, buy some and try them occasionally over the next few years. That way you'll know they're still edible and safe.

One five-gallon bucket full of 330 total servings of food sells for only about $100. One of my favorite products combines 950 meals with a fuel supply to heat them up. That one sells for about $500.

*** To maximize the longevity of your stored food, keep your food...

- Cool: 40 degrees Fahrenheit is optimal. For every 18-degree decrease, you double your food's storage life.
- Dry: A dry closet is a better storage location than a cooler, but damp, basement.
- Dark: Use opaque containers; ultraviolet light degrades nutritional value.
- Oxygen-free: Oxidation degrades nutritional value.
- Rotated: Follow the financial accountant's term "FIFO." It stands for "first in, first out." This makes stored food a simple extension of a regular consumption pattern.

*** One of the most exciting innovations in alternative agriculture is the field of hydroponics (also called "aquaponics"). If you have a backup power supply, you have the ability to grow nearly limitless supplies of food. You don't need soil or a conventional garden. And get this... hydroponic food grows about twice as fast as normal.

Hydroponics works by growing food vertically along the sides of five-foot towers. The roots of the plants are inside the towers, where they're bathed in recirculated water and air. It's a fascinating process. To learn more, I suggest you watch any of the many hydroponics videos available on YouTube.

Hydroponics is still in the do-it-yourself stage. Some kits have been made for consumer purchase. But because the field is still new, it's difficult to give a strong endorsement to one product over another. You can expect to pay $300-$500 for a premade kit. It may take a year to recoup your investment, but thereafter you have a renewable supply of fresh food.

You can get smaller kits on Amazon for $40-$60 each if you want to try it before fully commiting.

*** If you've lived through a hurricane, you've seen store shelves go bare as people rush to get emergency supplies. Below, I've listed the top 15 items that sell out first in a crisis. If you have these beforehand, you can avoid fighting frenzied crowds later.

1. Bottled Water
2. Pasta
3. Rice
4. Canned Soup
5. Canned Meats
6. Canned Vegetables
7. Canned Fruit
8. Popcorn
9. Salt
10. Condensed/Powdered Milk
11. Cereal
12. Beef Jerky
13. Grains
14. Cooking Oil
15. Sports Drinks

*** Lastly, don't forget about pets. If you have pets, they need to eat and drink as well. Some pets even need medicine. Stock up on these items just as you would for human necessities.

3. Power/Light. Now that you have food and water, it's helpful to have some form of backup power. This may range from heavy AC generators to small DC batteries. It all depends on the amount of power you would use during an extended outage.

The right gasoline-powered generator can provide all the electricity you need to maintain everyday living. You can power your lights, refrigerator, water heater, electric stoves, etc. Of course, this requires a great deal of fuel. When confronted with an outage of unknown duration, it's wise to conserve fuel by using the generator for bare necessities only.

*** If you are going to use a generator, keep the following basics in mind:

- **NEVER RUN A GENERATOR INSIDE THE HOUSE OR GARAGE.** Generators emit lethal fumes. These machines always require good ventilation.
- If you want to power your entire house with a generator, you'll need to install a transfer switch. This allows you to switch from normal electrical-grid power to your generator. A decent transfer switch costs around $500. Expect to pay a few hundred more to have it installed.
- 10-25 gallons of gasoline will provide one to two days of normal "on the grid" usage.
- Gasoline will degrade over time. So always add fuel stabilizer to stored gas.
- Store your gasoline in five-gallon cans. Keep the cans in a cool, safe place like a shed.
- Unplug all unnecessary appliances. Even when not turned on, devices like televisions, computers, and radios still draw electricity. (I do this when I travel for extended periods of time, too.)

*** There are several types and sizes of backup generators. They may be stationary or portable... They may run on gasoline, diesel fuel, propane, or natural gas... And they provide various wattages of electric power.

Most people elect to go with portable, gasoline-powered generators. They tend to provide the greatest flexibility and power for the lowest cost. Still, there are many choices here...

You must first determine how much wattage you require. A 5,000-watt generator should suffice for most homes. The nonprofit product-review company Consumer Reports provides a free wattage calculator. You can access it here: http://is.gd/WKpHgl

In the 5,000-watt category, units range from $500 to $3,000. Like any product, higher price does not necessarily equate to highest quality...

The Troy-Bilt XP 7000 30477 gasoline generator earned top honors from Consumer Reports in 2012. It put out up to 7,000 watts for 15 hours on its nine-gallon tank. The unit costs $900.

But the best value may be the Generac GP5500 5939. It came in a close third to a model that costs $2,800. But the Generac costs only around $700 and has almost identical functionality and longevity as the second-place model. Unless you know you need a 7,000-watt output, this 5,500-watt generator is your best buy.

*** Always keep flashlights and extra batteries on hand. When storing flashlights, store them with the batteries removed. Connected batteries lose charge faster and may corrode.

Store your alkaline and lithium batteries at room temperature, out of direct sunlight, and in a dry area... NOT in the refrigerator. Moisture from inside the fridge can reduce shelf life and performance. Alkaline batteries should have about a seven-year shelf life as they only lose about 1% per year at room temperature. Lithium batteries may last up to 15 years on the shelf.

Nickel batteries can be frozen, but they still lose about 10% a month in the freezer. These are often your rechargeable type battery.

A solid emergency flashlight should have a metal casing, adjustable beam, be brightly colored (easier to find in low-light conditions), have a lanyard, and contain a spare light bulb in its base. Larger flashlights that utilize C- or D-size batteries can flood more light into a dark space. Newer light-emitting diode (LED) flashlights put out a ton of light and can run on smaller AA-size batteries.

*** Lithium batteries beat alkaline batteries in terms of shelf life (15 years vs. seven years) and power output. But they are also more expensive. Energy-intensive devices like cameras and mp3 players need the extra power lithium batteries provide. Most flashlights do just fine with alkaline.

Consumer Reports ranks "Energizer Ultimate" lithium batteries as the best for both power output and longevity... but they're more than twice as expensive as their closest alkaline competitors.

Whatever you choose to use for batteries, follow the same rotation system. Stock up on batteries, then draw replacements from your stockpile. Again, FIFO rules the day: "First in, first out."

*** Plastic glow sticks are another source of light. They contain two liquid chemicals that emit light when they come into contact. Snapping the glow stick starts this reaction.

For brighter light, place the glow stick in boiling water. This speeds up the chemical reaction and produces brighter light output. It also reduces glow stick life. The opposite is true as well... placing activated glow sticks in ice slows the reaction and allows more time for illumination. Glow sticks can stay illuminated for several minutes to several hours, depending on the type. Check the labeling.

*** Candles may be used for lighting, but be mindful of the high risk of unintended fire. Always keep in mind the following candle safety tips:

- Never let a burning candle out of your sight. Always extinguish candles when exiting a room or going to sleep.

- Keep candles away from all flammable objects like curtains, furniture, books, paintings, etc.

- Trim candlewicks to one-quarter inch before burning. Crooked and long wicks cause uneven burning and dripping... an easy way to spread fire.

- Keep candles away from drafts, vents, and air currents.

- Never use a candle for light when fueling equipment like a kerosene lantern or gas generator.

- Be sure to have a charged fire extinguisher ready at all times.

*** If you have gas appliances, gas may flow, but electronic ignition switches will not work. Keep matches and/or a portable propane lighter ready to light the gas.

*** Unplug electronics not plugged into a surge protector. When the power comes back on, it may surge and damage this equipment. Keep one light switched "on" so you know when the power comes back online.

*** Some devices are "hand-crank" and require only "elbow grease" to function. This includes hand-crank flashlights and radios. You can even buy small hand-crank power generators (like the K-Tor Pocket Socket) that can recharge smart phones and tablet computers. These represent the ultimate "failsafe" in a no-power environment. The K-Tor unit sells for about $60 on Amazon.com.

I keep in my car a "shakable" flashlight that provides 1.5 minutes of light for about three minutes of shaking. The motion from driving keeps it charged.

*** Solar panels are another potential energy source, but their effectiveness is limited. Winter months, overcast days, night hours, and size constraints all limit solar power generation. They are also expensive. I do not recommend using solar power as your primary backup.

4. Communications. In the information age, a power outage also causes an information outage... and with it, a screeching halt to our way of life.

Communications companies often have backup generators. Cell networks and conventional "land lines" *may or may not* stay available during an extended power outage... And regardless, cell networks are useless if your cell phone is dead.

You may want to purchase a battery-operated cell phone charger. These should cost no more than $20 and provide up to 10 hours of talk time and 12 days of standby time. These chargers require lithium batteries.

Solar-powered cell phone chargers may also be an option. Check Amazon.com for the best selection. They start at around $25. But again, solar power has its limits.

*** Use a battery-powered or hand-crank radio to stay informed during the emergency. Emergency broadcasts from civil defense agencies will go out over AM radio stations.

Shortwave, civilian band (CB), and police/fire "scanner" radios are some other alternative communication devices. Uniden makes a wide variety of "alternative" radios. The company also has a good reputation for quality. A solid unit will cost you around $150.

*** Use cell phones for calling and texting only. Disable the "vibrate" feature if engaged, and don't watch video. Both accelerate battery depletion.

5. Emergency Contacts. Keep a hard-copy list of important phone numbers. This includes family, friends, neighbors, workplaces, and schools.

If you have school-age children, plan on who will pick them up in advance. Schools will not release custody of children to just anyone, even if they are relatives or family friends. Learn what these policies are ahead of time so you are prepared.

*** Below is a list of "must-have" numbers. Your list may be longer. Keep a copy of these numbers on paper. DO NOT just rely on an electronic device.

6. Money. ATMs and credit cards may be useless during an extended crisis. Always keep at least one week's worth of expenses on hand in cash. Keep it in a secure, hidden location. Tell only one other trusted family member where you've hidden your "stash."

Never brag to others about keeping wads of cash or other valuables in your home. It can make your house a local burglar's No. 1 target during a crisis. Remember the old wartime warning: "Loose lips sink ships." They also get your house robbed...

- Nearest relative outside of immediate family
- Local contact outside of family
- Nonlocal contact
- Nearest fire station
- Nearest police/sheriff department
- Nearest/preferred hospital
- Family doctor

- Pharmacy
- Poison control
- Red Cross
- Electric company
- Gas company
- Water/sanitation department
- Telephone/cable company
- Insurance agent
- Babysitter

*** Some people may also choose to conduct trade using silver coins during an extended crisis. "Junk silver" coins are U.S. quarters and dimes minted prior to 1965. The coins are 90% silver.

A $50 face-value bag of junk silver coins contains about 36 ounces of silver, in circulated, pre-1965 quarters and dimes. At the time of this writing, a $50 bag costs about $634. Check cointrackers.com for an up-to-the minute update of junk silver prices

You can find many reputable coin and bullion dealers across America, but many unscrupulous ones as well. If you mention junk silver and the dealer tries to sell you numismatic (collectible) coins instead, look elsewhere.

Buying silver and gold can be risky business if you do not know with whom you are dealing. Here are a few folks who "hoard" pre-1965 silver coins... and feel free to tell them we sent you. (We receive no compensation for mentioning them.)

Rich Checkan - Asset Strategies International
1700 Rockville Pike, Suite 400, Rockville, MD 20852
Phone: 800-831-0007 or 301-881-8600
Fax: 301-881-1936 E-mail: rcheckan@assetstrategies.com

Parker Vogt - Camino Coin
1301 Broadway Ave., Burlingame, CA 94010
Phone: 800-348-8001 or 650-348-3000
E-mail: Parker@caminocompany.com

The Doctor's Protocol Step No. 2: PROVISION.

STEP THREE
🛡 PROTECT

Step No. 1 of my Doctor's Protocol – PREPARE – showed you the fundamental skills necessary to survive any crisis… by having a well-trained, confident mind. This short-circuits the "negative panic" instinct and allows you take decisive action when you can still save yourself.

Then, in Step No. 2: PROVISION, we addressed things you need to have on hand to defend your life and well-being.

In Step No. 3: PROTECT, we'll show you more of the specific threats to your safety and how to protect yourself. Let me break these down into a little more detail here…

I conceive of threats in two ways:

1. Internal Threats
2. External Threats

It may sound basic, but people often go astray here. They end up putting most of their effort into defending against only one type of threat, the internal ones… while completely ignoring the other type. This is a recipe for failure.

Let's look at this distinction in terms of a simple car analogy.

Road Warrior

Every time you drive your vehicle, you face a slew of internal and external threats… both types can prevent you from reaching your desired destination.

Internal threats include things like running out of gas, never changing the engine oil, or driving on bald tires. It's only a matter of time before one of these threats breaks down your vehicle.

You can defend against these by taking preventative measures ahead of time. You keep the tank full, change the oil at regular intervals, buy new tires when needed. As you can see, you avoid most internal threats through proper provision.

External threats originate from outside the car. They can be just as problematic and often more acute.

A reckless driver might crash into you. Nails in the road can cause flats. Lousy mechanics may gouge you for shoddy work. You might even wake up one day to find a thief has stolen your car.

To defend against external threats, we need to create a strong shield.

We can take defensive driving classes. We can get recommendations before letting just anyone work on the vehicle. We can purchase run-flat tires and car alarms.

We can't predict every external threat. But we can prepare for the most likely ones. And many times, preparations to handle these threats can still protect us against unforeseen ones.

Know Thyself, Know The Crisis, Know Thy Enemy

I strongly believe the most critical external threats are germs, injury, violence, and exposure. Each one of these has the potential to cause serious harm and even death in a short amount of time. That's why it's crucial to raise an effective shield against them.

1. Germs. Everyone knows water is vital for hydration purposes. But I believe water provides an equally valuable benefit to us in sanitation. Never forget, disease is the No. 1 killer in the Third World. Disease is rampant there because of inadequate sanitation.

Fecal matter attracts flies and other vermin. Flies then land on food, doorknobs, skin, etc. Bacteria and other diseases spread. We end up touching it... and eventually ingesting it. That's why it's so critical to always wash your hands. A quick touch to the nose, eyes, or mouth is all it takes to infect yourself.

A crisis that leads to an extended power outage may disrupt your water pressure. This means you get one last flush and then... nothing. This can become a health issue in a hurry.

*** You can repurpose water used in cooking and cleaning to flush toilets. Collect all used water in a reservoir (like a rubber trash can). You can then use this water (via gallon jugs) for bathroom flushing.

When repurposing used water for flushing, *pour the water directly into the bowl, not the tank.* Soap and other particles may damage the tank's flushing mechanism. And don't worry. Increased vacuum pressure and gravity will cause the bowl to flush on its own.

*** If you run out of water to repurpose for sanitation, you still have other bathroom options. Use duct tape to fix a plastic bag to the inside of the toilet bowl to capture solid waste. Seal and double-bag the waste when finished. Store the sealed waste in a safe container (like a garbage bin) or bury underground. **Do not leave waste exposed. It will attract flies and spread disease.**

You can also turn a five-gallon bucket into a makeshift "potty" using the "tape and bag" method described above. If you don't want to seal up the bag after each use, you can cover the waste with wood ashes or quicklime (calcium-oxide powder, available at gardening stores).

Remember to:

- Completely cover the waste after each use.
- Keep a lid over the top of the bucket.
- Seal up and dispose of the bags after they are no more than half full.

*** I'm not a fan of hand sanitizer in general. It's more dangerous than soap and helps grow strains of drug-resistant germs. Under normal circumstances, I don't use it. However, I do keep a backup bottle for emergencies, just in case I'm without clean water for an extended period of time.

*** Keep bleach, ammonia, and/or distilled vinegar on hand to clean plumbing fixtures, buckets, and other surfaces.

*** If you've run completely out of fresh water, you still have a backup. It may sound miraculous, but you can generate water right out of the air. It's free and easy to do, if you know what you're doing. You can make a "solar still."

Here's what to do:

- In the morning, dig a hole two-feet deep and place a cup in the middle.
- Harvest green leaves, green branches, and green grass.
- Fill the hole with these fresh, green materials, no higher than the lip of the cup.
- Place a clear plastic sheet or garbage bag flat over the top of the hole. Secure the sides of the plastic with dirt or other weights.
- Place a small stone in the middle of the plastic, so it sags and the lowest part rests over the cup.
- Allow the still to work over the course of day.

By the evening, moisture from the green vegetation will have evaporated, collected on the plastic sheet, and dripped down into the cup.

You have fresh water for drinking and washing, harvested "from thin air." The water itself will be clean, no need for sterilization. If you can't be sure the cup or the plastic were uncontaminated, you should sterilize the water first. But if you know the cup and plastic are clean, the water itself will be ready to drink.

*** You can buy machines that do this too. They're called "atmospheric water generators." Of course, you need backup power to run them in a crisis. If you are interested in learning more, I suggest you look here: www.ecoloblue.com

The cheapest unit goes for $1,300 and can produce up to eight gallons of fresh water per day, depending on your location. The more humid your location, the more water it will produce.

2. Injury and Other Medical Considerations. You can avoid a great deal of infection and illness through good sanitary conditions. Of course, when infection or injury does happen, you want to be prepared. Use the information that follows to manage these threats.

*** The most important thing you MUST do when sustaining a scratch or open wound is clean the wound thoroughly. Use soap and vigorously scrub the area to remove all dirt and organisms. It won't feel pleasant... but it is vital to preventing infection. After you've cleaned the wound, apply an antiseptic ointment like Neosporin and cover with a bandage. Repeat this process daily until the wound heals.

*** When an infected person sneezes, they atomize harmful bodily fluids. Wearing "N95-grade" medical masks will reduce the transmission of fluid-borne diseases. Use these to keep illness from spreading throughout your family. You can buy a 30-pack of these masks for around $10.

*** Keep a supply of antibacterial (hand sanitizer) gel on hand to prevent infections and transmission of disease in crises. Water for washing and disinfecting may be shut off or nonpotable for an extended time.

*** You'll want your immune system working at peak capacity to ward off infection. A healthy diet, ample sleep (seven hours or more per night), and regular exercise maintain your immunity... but these things may be impossible in a crisis.

This is a case where multivitamin tablets will help you. Regular readers know I often warn of the dangers of ingesting too many vitamin supplements... But in a disaster situation, taking one multivitamin tablet every day throughout the crisis will ensure you're getting an adequate supply of micronutrients and consumed much faster under stress.

As always, I recommend people take vitamin C if they feel an illness coming on. Also try to get ample vitamin D naturally from direct sunlight for at least 20 minutes a day or keep a supply of inexpensive vitamin D3 supplements for the winter months.

*** Many people are accustomed to accessing the Internet to gain instant knowledge on an almost infinite array subjects. This includes help on how to treat sickness and dress injuries. But in a crisis, we may not have access to the Internet.

It's still important to keep at least two "real" medical volumes (hardcopy, not electronic "e-books") on hand. My top recommendation is *Wilder-*

ness Medicine. The *PDR Pharmacopoedia Pocket Dosing Guide* and the *Village Health Care Handbook* are also excellent.

*** If you are taking prescription drugs, maintain a surplus of at least two weeks of prescription drugs. Work with your doctor to get insurance companies to pay for the extra meds. One way to do this is to ask for a 90-day supply through a pharmacy benefits management plan. Then, ask your doctor for more a few weeks early, say at 60 days. Rotate these prescription drugs into your regular consumption in the same way you would with stored food and water.

*** Maintain a ready supply of antibiotics. I recommend Augmentin, Ciprofloxin ("Cipro"), Doxycycline, and Bactrim (from the sulfa family). **Make sure you are not allergic to any these antibiotics before taking them.**

Talk with your doctor now about how to get these drugs. He or she may have free trial packs (like the popular "Z-Pac") to share with you.

Doctors will often prescribe Cipro and Bactrim DS (both as generics) for people planning overseas trips. You can get 60 pills (a one-month supply) of each at Wal-Mart for $20 or a 10-day supply for $10. Rite Aid sells generic Doxycycline for a similar price.

Store these drugs in a sealed freezer bag with desiccant (anti-moisture) packets inside. Place them in the freezer. Once thawed, they will last for 10 to 12 months when kept at room temperature.

*** Be certain you have plenty of anti-diarrhea medicine, like Pepto-Bismol. Pepto in tablet form is best. Diarrhea is the fastest way to become dehydrated... so always err on the side of more Pepto, not less. I also keep a few bottles of ginger ale and potassium pills on hand to prevent severe dehydration.

Extensive vomiting or diarrhea can leave you weak, thirsty, and with depleted potassium levels. If it goes on too long, it can be a serious health threat. The sugar in the soda gives some calories. The ginger is a natural anti-emetic. (It calms the stomach.) And the potassium pills restore that chemical's levels.

Do what I've said and add the potassium to ginger ale and let it dissolve. Potassium pills are hard to "stomach" and since you already feel icky, don't worsen it.

*** If you have elderly, ill, young, or infirm family members in your home, contact your utility company and inform them of this before an outage occurs. Power company crews should give your home higher priority when working to reestablish power.

*** Keep an extra supply of special batteries on hand for devices like hearing aids and electric scooters.

*** Keep a first-aid kit with bandages, antiseptic, and ointment at the ready. Any decent first-aid kit should have the following minimum components. Your kit may have more.

- Latex gloves
- Bandages (small, medium, large, and butterflies; 10 of each)
- Gauze pads
- First-aid tape (at least 3 rolls)
- Elastic "ACE" bandage
- Triple-antibiotic ointment (like Neosporin)
- Topical antiseptic towelettes
- 1- to 4-oz bottle of povidone-iodine 10% solution (for disinfecting wounds)
- Pain/anti-inflammatory medication (e.g., Tylenol, ibuprofen, etc.)
- Anti-diarrheal and laxative tablets (Lomotil and Pepto-Bismol for diarrhea)
- Cough drops
- Sunscreen (keep SPF 30 in case you have to be outside during the middle of the day for emergencies)
- Tweezers
- Scissors
- Scalpel or single-edge razor blades
- Matches and bottle of rubbing alcohol (for sterilizing instruments)
- Antibiotics (ask your doctor for help stocking up... and make sure you are not allergic to the drugs)
- Duct tape (at least 3 rolls)
- A quality first-aid handbook
- A box of quicklime (for human waste)
- A box of garbage bags

A wide variety of prepackaged first-aid kits exists... but they can get expensive. You can find a quality first-aid kit that includes most (or all) of the items above for a reasonable price. For example, Phoenix-Lazarus makes one of the best first-aid kits I've found. It sells for around $30. Check for it on Amazon.com. Be sure to buy the other items it doesn't include.

*** At least one person in your family should be trained in basic first-aid and CPR (cardio-pulmonary resuscitation). Getting every family member certified is better. Check with the Red Cross, a nearby fire station, or your local community college for class offerings.

The "new" CPR (or "hands only" CPR) says chest compressions are the most important thing to do... As long as airways are open, focus on consistent chest compression. Watch the one-minute video "Official 2012 Hands-Only CPR Instructional Video" on YouTube to learn more.

*** CPR is not the only lifesaving skill you should know. Three other simple techniques can save lives in emergencies.

The first is called the "Three-Fourths Prone" or "recovery" position. If you have restarted normal breathing through CPR, placing the victim into this position is the next step. It protects an unconscious patient by keeping blood, saliva, vomit, and their tongue out of the way. You can learn how to do it by watching the two-minute video from the Epilepsy Society "Recovery Position: Step by Step Guide" on YouTube.

You also need to know how to stop bleeding. Do this by applying consistent, firm pressure on top of a clean cloth or sturdy paper towel (how fibers help clot blood) to the wound for 15 minutes. The pressure should not be so strong that it cuts off all circulation. And don't remove it.

If that is not adequate to stem blood flow, press along the upstream artery (at a location closer to the heart) while keeping pressure on the wound itself. You can learn more by watching this three-minute how-to video: "How to Stop Bleeding" from Howcast on YouTube.

If these techniques still can't stop the bleeding, the last resort is to apply a tourniquet. Wrap a length of rope or belt around the bleeding limb (at a location closer to the heart). This is a last resort because it cuts off circulation to the whole limb and the limb may be lost. The video, "First Aid and Safety Procedures: How to Make and Apply a Tourniquet." on YouTube will teach you more.

3. Violence and Physical Safety. In an extended crisis, it doesn't take long before unprepared people start to wonder where their next meal, tank of gas, or swig of clean water is going to come from. Those who are relaxed in "regular" life may become desperate in an emergency. And those who are already predatory become even more emboldened to encroach on others.

Even in "normal" times, it's rare for the police to prevent a crime... They can only respond to them after they occur. Today, the cops in Detroit take an average of 58 minutes to respond to a call. Imagine, in a time of civil unrest, the police may never come at all. There won't be enough cops to answer every emergency call.

I believe the absolute best way to handle conflict is to avoid it in the first place. Anything that can be done to defuse a situation is always preferable to an actual fight. There is just too much at risk for too little reward.

*** **Burglary** is still a major threat to the safety of you and your family. With more than 47 million Americans needing taxpayer assistance (food stamps) just to eat, many people are desperate. They may target your home for invasion and burglary... even with you inside it.

Jack MacLean is a former burglar. He stole more than $133 million in jewels in his career as a thief. After his arrest and conviction, he decided to reform. In prison, he interviewed some 300 other burglars about their preferred tricks and tactics. He compiled what he learned in his book, *Secrets of a Superthief.*

It turns out 100% of the burglars admitted that one technique would scare them away from a property in an instant...

They all were afraid of one blast from an extremely loud air horn.

Search online or go to your local marine supply store. You can buy an air horn for around $20. Be sure to buy the $20 model... $10 horns are not loud enough. Falcon makes ideal marine horns.

Simple, safe techniques like this are the preferred approach to stopping a threat. The threat disappears, and no one gets hurt.

*** Defense experts all agree: Self-defense starts with a mental readiness to take action. Do whatever is in your power to avoid conflict... but if you cannot escape a physical altercation, commit yourself to inflicting maximum damage on your attacker quickly. The goal is to end the conflict and exit the situation as soon as possible.

No matter the size or look of your assailant, all humans have the same vulnerable spots: the eyes, throat, knees, and groin. Commit yourself to attacking these weak spots with full force – fingers to the eyes, kicks to the knees and groin, punches to the throat – and then get out of there.

*** Prepare yourself ahead of time by taking self-defense classes. Avoid martial arts courses that focus on competition or teach a sport. These may be great exercise and an enjoyable pastime... but you don't want to compete with a would-be attacker. You want to disable him and leave the situation.

One of the most famous forms of this no-nonsense, life-saving, self-defense approach is Krav Maga (http://www.kravmaga.com/).

*** Burglar alarms and "panic buttons" will not function during an extended power outage. Enhance your self-defense capabilities by arming yourself. I'll show you my recommendations below.

*** Tasers are a weapon I don't care to own. They are expensive (up to $1,000 for one that "shoots"). And even though they are considered "less-than-lethal," people have died from getting "tased." I'd rather avoid all the risks.

*** I am a fan of "all-in-one" utility knives... You'd be amazed how handy they can be. And of course, that includes using them for self-defense, should the need arise.

Gerber makes my favorite utility knife. It includes scissors, pliers, files, and multiple blades. The Gerber "Dime" sells for around $18 on Amazon.com.

*** My preferred self-defense armament should be on the end of every keychain... and in the drawer of a bedroom nightstand. It's a small canister of pepper spray. It's only three-inches tall, but can shoot a chemical stream six to 12 feet. The chemicals inside are the same formula used by bounty hunters and law enforcement. And it sells for a little more than $10 on Amazon.

*** Skillful, safe use of firearms will go a long way in ensuring your family's safety. It's important to equip yourself with the right hardware and ammunition. And *you need to know how to use it...*

Handguns are more convenient for close-quarters situations. Shotguns are the "heavy artillery" that will stop almost any living creature in its tracks – forever. You can choose from a nearly infinite variety of firearms. But for personal safety and emergency preparation, the most important factors are stopping power and personal comfort.

With handguns, I recommend at least .45-caliber weapons. Something smaller may not stop a crazed or drug-induced attacker. With shotguns, I recommend a 12-gauge weapon (nothing less than the smaller 20-gauge). Choose "double-ought" (00) buckshot for shotgun ammunition.

*** Weapons like these are much more expensive than horns or pepper spray. A solid .45-caliber Automatic Colt Pistol (ACP) handgun sells for less than $1,000. (Some are far cheaper.) A good 12-gauge, pump-action shotgun will set you back no more than $500.

If this is your first gun purchase, modern gun and sporting goods stores have knowledgeable and courteous staff ready to assist you. A few examples are Cabelas (www.cabelas.com), Able Ammo (www.ableammo.com), and Midway (www.midwayusa.com).

*** When it comes to purchasing weapons confidentially, conducting a private transaction (i.e., not with a registered gun dealer) is the way to go. In general, an individual may buy or sell a weapon from/to another individual in the same state without any official record of the transaction. Check your state laws for unique restrictions that may or may not apply to you and the other party.

One venue that facilitates these types of transactions is a local "gun show." If you've never attended one of these events, you should... even if you have no intention of purchasing a weapon. You can learn a huge amount about emergency preparedness (of all sorts)... while remaining anonymous.

*** Most important of all, if you buy a handgun or shotgun, **train yourself in the safe operation of these weapons.** They should feel like extensions of your hands, just like a car feels like an extension of your body... you don't even think about driving, you just react. You want to be as familiar and at-ease with your firearm or other weapon as you are with your car (another deadly weapon if abused).

Many of the stores that sell weapons also offer training programs. Other private schools exist as well. One of the best is called Front Sight (www.frontsight.com) in Nevada. Military and police forces from around the U.S. send personnel to this private academy.

4. Exposure. Modern conveniences have improved human life so much, creature comforts have become a given. Even a destitute individual can drink unlimited, free, clean, ice-cold water from a fountain on a hot summer day.

But an extended power outage can shake us from this dreamlike existence in a flash. When the air conditioning or central heating unit goes down, the elements remind us just how dangerous they can be. Whether you are at home or outdoors, you need to know how to defend against the threat of exposure to the elements.

*** The U.S. Air Force sends all airmen who may get shot down over hostile territory to SERE school. SERE stands for Survival, Evasion, Resistance, and Escape. The course instructors pound two numbers into the heads of their trainees.

The first number is 98.6 (degrees Fahrenheit). That's a human's normal operating temperature. It must be your first thought in fighting the elements. Do whatever is necessary to stay as close to this temperature as possible. In the section below, I'll share with you some techniques to do this. But for now, remember that maintaining 98.6 is your No. 1 priority.

*** There are some easy ways to keep your body temperature as close to 98.6 F as possible.

If you are overheating, get out of direct sunlight. Wear loose-fitting cotton clothes. Apply water (or any liquid) to the forehead, neck (front and back), inner elbows (where they bend), and back of the knees.

Water evaporation is an exothermic reaction. This means it dissipates heat as it evaporates. Blowing on or fanning the moistened regions will accelerate the process.

If you are trying to keep warm, apply as many layers as possible. Your body stays warm by heating the air trapped beneath the layers. Stuff crumpled paper into your pockets and in between the layers. The extra insulation provides more air pockets to trap heat.

You can also fashion an improvised sleeping bag out of crumpled papers and two large garbage bags. Place one bag inside the other. Then fill the space between the two bags with crumpled paper.

The second critical number is 3... They call it the "Rule of 3." It helps you keep your survival priorities in order.

The Rule of 3 states you **cannot** survive...

- 3 seconds without spirit and hope

- 3 minutes without air

- 3 hours without shelter in extreme conditions

- 3 days without water

- 3 weeks without food

- 3 months without companionship or love

When you find yourself exposed to the elements, bear in mind the Rule of 3. It will help you prioritize which disaster responses to implement first.

*** The first big jump in survival longevity in the Rule of 3 occurs after you have secured water... from three days to three weeks.

One of the best products I have ever seen is called LifeStraw. It's a personal water filter. You can stick one end in a stagnant, dirty pond and suck in safe, clean, filtered drinking water – instantly.

It can filter up to at least 265 gallons of drinkable water in its life cycle. But take note, it will not desalinate water. You can't use it to drink from the ocean.

The LifeStraw fits in your pocket. I keep one in my car's glove box. If you are left stranded and exposed, few things could come in handier. It sells for around $20 on Amazon.

The Doctor's Protocol Step No. 3: PROTECT

STEP FOUR
$ PROSPER

Up to this point in the Doctor's Protocol, we've discussed critical steps you need to take to survive any number of emergencies. If you've followed the steps I've described, you and your family are now safer than at least 95% of the general public. That's pretty good, but if you're like me...

It's not good enough.

When I buy insurance on my life, I like to have 100% coverage. That's why I've included Step No. 4: PROSRER in my Protocol. It's the final step you need to round out a fully integrated, 360-degree approach to emergency preparedness.

General Quarters

If you ever get the chance to visit a Navy ship, I suggest you do it. Non-profit organizations have converted several vessels into museums around the United States. Once aboard, you get the sense of how dangerous it is to operate a warship.

Even under peaceful conditions, ships are loaded with explosive ordinance and dangerous machinery (like nuclear reactors). Just one sailor's carelessness could send everyone to the bottom. That's why readiness is fundamental and training is a constant activity on board.

My Navy friends have described to me an order called "general quarters." It is a command to bring the ship to a state of maximum battle readiness. It takes only a couple minutes.

When the bridge sounds "GQ," crew members stop everything and rush to their battle stations. They don protective gear. They bring weapons systems online. They seal all watertight doors and hatches (openings between decks). The ship and crew are made ready to face all threats.

Unfortunately, things may still go wrong. Some crises are just too overwhelming. That's why every watertight hatch has a smaller, circular hatch in the center.

It's called an "escape scuttle."

In the worst-case scenario, the crew still needs to be prepared to abandon ship. They'll climb up through the escape scuttles, out to the life rafts... and live to fight another day.

Know Thyself, Know the Crisis, Know thy Enemy, Know Thy Escape

As I've said before, we shouldn't try to plan for every conceivable bad thing that may happen. It's impossible. And it's a bad way to live life. That why we've used common sense and statistics to refine our readiness strategy and tactics.

Still, the work we did in the first three steps would be useless if we did not also have an escape hatch. Consider it a backup for our backup. Steps 1-3 have helped us engineer a degree of readiness worthy of a battleship... but we still need to be ready to hit the escape scuttle if the worst case happens.

This means being able to transport your life and assets to a new location at a moment's notice. The good news is, it's easier than you think... if you prepare properly first.

1. Life. The digital age has made recordkeeping easier than ever before. This is a double-edged sword. Digital recordkeeping allows tremendous ease in transporting and accessing your entire "digital life." But digital records also make your identity easy to "hack," steal, and exploit.

You can take some simple steps now to transfer all your important records into digital form. Remember, the most important part is to **safeguard this digital information.** I'll show you how in a moment.

But first, recognize there is an inverse relationship between information accessibility and information security. The more secure you make your information, the less accessible it tends to be (and vice versa). It takes extra effort to make your records both accessible and secure at the same time.

*** You can easily put all of your papers, photos, financial documents, passwords, and important policies on a high-capacity gigabyte "flash drive."

If you're not familiar with these, flash drives are the size of your pinky finger. They plug into any computer and can store more information than computers that were built just a few years ago.

You can buy a super-rugged flash drive made by Kingston with up to 512 gigabytes (GB) of storage space. This is probably big enough to store EVERY photo, movie, video, and piece of paper in your house.

Keep in mind that a 1 GB drive can store about 500 photos on average... so we're talking about something the size of your little finger that could store, approximately:

- 25,000 photos
- 25,000 pages of documents
- 13,000 songs
- 40 movies
- 600 minutes of family videos...

And still not even be half full!

You can put your critical flash drive in your pocket or wear it around your neck, at a moment's notice. This way – even in the absolute worst-case scenario in which you have to leave your home for an extended period – you've still got everything you really need, in one simple place.

The Kingston 512 GB flash drive sells for $630, and the 256 GB drive goes for $330 on Amazon.

And remember, be sure to encrypt all sensitive information on your flash drive. I'll tell you more about how to do this next.

*** The downside to putting your digital life on a single flash drive is that you may lose track of it... and with it, your entire-digital life. But if you put it in a safe, you might not be able to get to it before needing to evacuate at a moment's notice. (Called "bugging out.")

An alternative way to store your data is to utilize "cloud computing." Companies like Apple and Microsoft offer free storage space (up to around 10 GB per account) on their own servers. You can then access any file stored "in the cloud" from any device with an Internet connection. The danger, of course, is putting sensitive information into third-party hands.

Do NOT upload your most important personal files unencrypted into the cloud.

If you encrypt your files FIRST, this may be an acceptable way of storing your data. You can download free, easy-to-use programs like TrueCrypt or Box-Cryptor to protect your data. Only then should you upload them to the cloud, place them on a flash drive, or even store them on your own computer.

You can learn more about these programs here: http://is.gd/kxjPuL.

Remember, if it's important and in digital form, please encrypt it.

*** If you want to double-down on encryption, you can choose a cloud service like Kim Dotcom's (yes, that's his legal name) storage site "Mega." The service offers 50 GB of free cloud storage per account. If you want more storage space, you can get up to 4 terabytes (TB) – 1 TB equals 1,000 GB – of storage for less than $40 per month.

The added bonus is Mega encrypts everything uploaded onto its servers. Only you have the encryption key. So the folks running this service couldn't spy on your information even if they wanted to. And if a snooping government wanted your files, they would still only get encrypted data.

As you can imagine, this has made Mega a target of the U.S. government and the Hollywood entertainment complex (even though it's in New Zealand). You should be aware of the firestorm surrounding the site if you decide to use it. You can access Mega here: https://mega.co.nz/.

As long as you encrypt your sensitive information *before* uploading it to one of the big-name cloud sites like Apple's iCloud or Microsoft's Skydrive, you should be fine. You can be sure these companies and their services will be around for a long time to come.

If you want even extra security through "double encryption," you may want to consider using Mega. Just be aware that there is a risk the site may be taken down by angry governments.

*** No matter how you decide to store your digital life, remember this important point with encryption: Once it's encrypted, you must remember the encryption key (password). There is no way to reset it. *If you forget it, those files are gone.*

I've written about the easy way to create and memorize complicated passwords in my special report, "The Easy Way to Maintain Your Privacy in America." You should also keep a hard-copy backup of your passwords in a safe or another hidden location.

2. Assets. If you ever have to "get out of Dodge" in a hurry, it would be best to do so with more than the shirt on your back (and flash drive in your pocket). Fortunately, there are easy ways to take a substantial portion of your wealth with you. As always, the important thing is to have prepared ahead of time.

*** Gold is usually considered the most valuable form of money to have when leaving your home in a crisis. You can carry tens of thousands of dollars in a few gold coins in your pockets. No one will be the wiser.

In Step No. 2: PROVISION, I mentioned that silver is great for conducting "routine" crisis transactions, like buying food. But is not optimal for travel. You would have to lug around conspicuous, large bags to take a large dollar amount with you. Gold avoids this problem.

As I warned before, many disreputable precious metals dealers are out there. Below are two dealers we trust...

Rich Checkan - Asset Strategies International
1700 Rockville Pike, Suite 400
Rockville, MD 20852
Phone: 800-831-0007 or 301-881-8600
Fax: 301-881-1936
E-mail: rcheckan@assetstrategies.com

Parker Vogt - Camino Coin 1301 Broadway Ave.
Burlingame, CA 94010
Phone: 800-348-8001 or 650-348-3000
E-mail: Parker@caminocompany.com

(We receive no compensation from the endorsement.)

*** Many people believe bank wires and credit cards are the only way to transfer money. In actuality, you have many alternatives.

You can send large sums of cash to most places in the world via the U.S. postal service. It's legal, safe, and inconspicuous... if you follow these easy steps:

- Buy 50 business-size envelopes, 50 first-class stamps, and a magazine (one with lots of pictures is best)
- Wrap five $100 bills in one page of the magazine and seal them in an envelope
- Repeat 49 more times.
- Do NOT place extra tape along the flap or do anything to make the envelope stand out
- Mail these from different post offices, over a few days, if possible
- Total Cost: around $25
- Total Cash Sent: $25,000

Privacy expert J.J. Luna has used this technique for more than 25 years and has never lost a dollar in the process.

*** Global, anonymous "cash" transfers do exist, too. In the post-9/11 world, any transaction that happens outside of the banking system has been under attack. Of course, it's all being done in the name of "fighting terrorism." But there are still alternatives.

Hawala banking is an ancient means of transferring money anonymously. It began in the Middle East in the 8th century. It's still thriving in the modern world... for those who know where to find it. It works like this...

- You go to a "hawaladar" (hawala banker/broker).
- You give him, say, $25,000 in U.S. dollars and tell him you want to transfer it to your friend in Australia.

- He accepts your money and gives you a password.
- He also tells the password to his hawaladar counterpart in Australia.
- You then give the password to your friend in Australia.
- Your friend goes to the Australian hawaladar and tells him the password.
- The passwords match, and that hawaladar gives your friend the equivalent of $25,000 in Australian dollars.
- Both hawaladars take a small commission. They promise to settle up with each other at some point in the future.

This private money transfer system is 100% legal in the U.S. and around the world. The problem is, it can be difficult to find your local hawaladar. But if you are patient and resourceful, you can do it. The following websites can offer you a good starting point:

http://is.gd/ikYfAL

http://is.gd/fhXGY3

*** A great way to move assets out of the U.S. is to own real estate in a foreign country. Real estate is perhaps the best way of getting and keeping assets overseas. The reason is simple. It's not reportable. And if it generates no income, you pay no tax on it either. Some of the smartest folks I know invested in foreign real estate and now have millions of dollars in assets offshore and out of the reach of the U.S. government.

Also, several countries (Panama and Costa Rica, for example) allow you to invest in real estate and even sustainable timber farms. With enough money invested, you can get a permanent visa and even citizenship after five years with little or no questions asked. In addition, real estate can be made more liquid if you place it in a corporation or trust. This makes it easier to sell or transfer your assets.

The publications *International Living* and *Live and Invest Overseas* (both from our parent company, Agora) are two great resources for learning more about international real estate opportunities. You can learn more at their websites: www.internationalliving.com and www.liveandinvestoverseas.com.

Bullion gold and silver (and other metals) are another way to keep assets offshore. They're not reportable, nor do they generate taxable income until you sell them. So keeping bullion in a private and secure place overseas is a simple way to hold (and move) assets offshore.

Of course, that requires jetting around the globe with sacks of gold, which can create its own complications. An alternative is a "proof of ownership of bullion" issued in a certificate from the Perth Mint in Perth, Australia. These certificates – often referred to as "Perth Certs" – are legal, but not reportable since they are not considered foreign financial accounts. The mint stores your metal until you request delivery or stop by the mint in Australia to pick it up. You can easily buy thousands of dollars worth of gold in the U.S., travel to Panama, and put the certificates in a buried box, under your pillow, or even redeem the gold certificates for cash in the Panama City branch of the Perth Mint.

An official distributor of Perth Certs who can help you get started is Asset Strategies International. Call 800-831-0007 or 301-881-8600 and ask for Rich Checkan or Glen Kirsch. You can also send an e-mail to rcheckan@assetstrategies.com.

3. Transportation. If you've made the decision to relocate, you're going to need a way to get where you're going. In the items that follow, I'll show you what to do to make sure you can travel unimpeded.

*** If you have a safe place to store gasoline (like a cool shed), keep a five-gallon gas can filled at all times. Remember to add fuel stabilizer or the gas will spoil over time.

*** In general, it's wise to refill your car at the half tank or one-quarter tank mark. (I always refill at a half tank.) Don't wait until you're running on fumes. You never know when a sudden crisis may hit. You never want to be stuck in a two-mile, four-hour-long gas line full of frustrated people.

And if you know a major storm is approaching the area... fill up your vehicle's tank immediately.

*** Plan an evacuation route ahead of time. If you've been warned of an impending crisis (like a major storm), DO NOT WAIT TO EVACUATE. You do not want to hit the highway when everyone else does. It will sooner resemble a parking lot than an expressway.

*** If you need to travel somewhere on foot, you can use the "invisible man" technique...

Janitors, deliverymen, cable guys, and more all come and go every day without anyone giving them a second glance. You can buy used uniforms online, or check at your local thrift store. Wearing the disguise can help you get where you need to go without raising much attention.

*** Government personnel may block roads or escape routes in a crisis. This is another good reason to get CERT qualification (see Step No. 1: PREPARE). You'll have official identification. You'll also have a plausible reason for needing to get through whatever checkpoints may have been set up.

*** If you are single, the best form of transportation for escaping a crisis is an off-road motorcycle. A dirt bike lets you go a long way on one tank of gas. You can also take routes that cars cannot (and be able to ride between or around them when backups occur).

*** Always be sure to have a physical, paper roadmap for your area and where you plan to go. Most people don't have these anymore. I recommend getting a couple of your local area and state immediately. Smart phone and global positioning satellite (GPS) communications may be down in a crisis.

I keep a Gazetteer of my local states in my car. Delorme makes them for less than $20 and they show every route you can imagine, including elevation and terrain changes.

4. Location. Finally, you need someplace safe to go. Your two choices are basically foreign or domestic.

*** One of the benefits of buying property overseas is that you have a ready alternative home. If you plan to get there, make sure you and your family all have current passports ahead of time. For all information regarding passport applications, renewals, changes, etc., visit: http://travel.state.gov/passport/passport_1738.html.

*** If you do not have a foreign residence, you still have many domestic evacuation options.

Cities are usually the worst places to be in a crisis. You may want to buy a second home in a rural area. Farmland is another option. Farms carry the added benefit of producing food for consumption and trade.

*** If you cannot afford a second residence, you can ask relatives or friends who live in the countryside if you can stay with them during a crisis. They may even welcome the extra help and/or compensation you can provide during your stay.

*** You can also volunteer to help rural charities. They may be able to provide room and board in exchange for your service.

Again, the most important thing with all of these options is to prepare ahead of time.

5. Prosper. Once you've secured your life and liberty, you should be looking at the opportunity crises provide. Make no mistake, I'm NOT saying you should take advantage of others in a dire situation. One of the reasons you've prepared so well is to be able to help your family and everyone else you can in trying times. Being able to provide aid to those in need will enrich your life more than any fiscal dealings ever could.

Still, to the well-prepared, there are always beneficial financial opportunities available around a time of crisis. I've added the following special section – "How to Build a Fortune During a Panic or Crisis" to help you recognize and take advantage of these opportunities when they arise.

HOW TO BUILD A FORTUNE DURING A PANIC OR CRISIS

Do you run from crisis... or towards it?

In "real life," running away from crisis is often the right move.

For example, if your house is burning, the right move is to grab your family and run out of the house. If you're in an area where a massive hurricane is expected to hit, the right move is to get out of there immediately.

But when it comes to investing, *running away from crisis will cause you to miss the greatest deals of your life.*

If you see financial crises as a cause to run away – instead of buying with both hands – you'll always miss out on once-in-a-decade opportunities to build wealth.

This is true because after people move past the "freeze" stage of crisis reaction, **they sell first and ask questions later.** The average spooked investor sells and sells and sells with no regards to the underlying value of what he is selling. When people are spooked, they'll sell almost anything for almost any price.

If you've ever encountered someone who was desperate to sell something, you know that as a buyer, you're going to get a great price. It may sound calloused, but it's just the way it is...

A 688% Gain on One of the World's Safest Companies

When fear enveloped the market in late 2008, investors unloaded shares of Starbucks, one of the world's greatest businesses.

Terrified investors sold so heavily that Starbucks fell from a high of $37 per share to $8 a share. The extraordinary selloff left Starbucks trading for absurdly cheap levels relative to cash flows, assets, and growth trajectory.

Of course... the sun still came up, and the Apocalypse never came.

People kept flocking to their favorite local coffeehouse to buy $4 lattes. Starbucks kept minting money and kept growing.

Just a few years after bottoming around $8 per share during the 2008 panic, Starbucks traded for $63 per share... *a more than 688% gain.*

Desperate conditions create tremendous bargains.

For example, in late 2008, when investors were worried the credit crisis would cause "The Great Depression Part 2," they dumped shares of one of the world's greatest businesses, Coca-Cola.

During the crisis, panicked investors sold so heavily that Coke fell to $19.55 a share (from a high of a little less than $32 a share the year before). This huge bout of selling left Coke trading for extremely cheap levels relative to its assets and cash flows.

You know what happened afterwards: The "Great Depression Part 2" did not arrive.

Instead... people kept drinking their favorite soda. Coca-Cola kept growing and churning out profits. And just a few years after bottoming around $19 per share during the 2009 panic, Coke now trades for more than $40 per share... a more than 100% gain... on one of the largest, safest, "most boring" companies on the planet.

The big gain in Coke is not unique. Dozens of elite companies traded for very cheap prices in 2008 and 2009... and then skyrocketed when the storm clouds cleared. All it took to make extraordinary gains in these businesses was to run towards the crisis with cash in hand.

In this section, I'm going to show you my favorite way to use a crisis to build wealth. If you follow this simple strategy, you'll set yourself up for a lifetime of buying the world's best assets for extraordinary discounts...

Why You Should Keep a 'Shopping List' of the World's Best Businesses

When you think of Coca-Cola... or Starbucks... or McDonalds, what comes to mind?

If you're like hundreds of millions of people around the world, things like "treat"... "part of my daily routine"... or "crave" come to mind.

Hundreds of millions of people see these businesses as trusted brand names with consistent products that can be purchased almost anywhere.

That's why, when I think of elite companies like Coke, Starbucks, and McDonalds, I think of the word "blue chip."

If you're unfamiliar with the term, know that "blue chip" is the label given to world-class businesses that dominate their industries. (Remember... in a basic set of poker chips, the blue chips are the most valuable.)

Blue chips typically have extremely robust business models... high profit margins... big competitive advantages... and low debt levels.

These attributes make blue chips the safest stocks in the world... and perfect for conservative investors.

Blue-chip stocks are the stock market's equivalent of beachfront property.

Beachfront property is always in demand. It resists down markets better than undesirable locations. It's the best.

I'm sure you've used the products and services of many blue-chip businesses...

You've probably enjoyed a coffee at Starbucks... or a soda made by Coca-Cola... or french fries from McDonalds. You've probably used a computer with software by Microsoft. You've probably covered a cut with a Band-Aid from Johnson & Johnson. You've probably fueled your car at a gas station owned by ExxonMobil.

When you can buy these beachfront-property stocks for fire-sale prices – the kind of prices available during crisis times – you should buy as much of them as you can afford.

That's why I like to keep a "shopping list" of the world's best blue-chip businesses. When a crisis makes these businesses cheap, I buy them... and look to hold them for years. And I place a special emphasis on blue chips that pay regular dividends. That's because...

'Dividends Don't Lie'

A dividend is a distribution of a company's earnings. It's a way for the owners of a company to collect an immediate return on their investment.

Dividends are often quoted in terms of the "yield" they offer investors.

For example, if a stock has a share price of $10 and pays a $0.50-per-share annual dividend, the "dividend yield" is 5%.

Smart, sophisticated investors have a saying about these payments made to shareholders: "Dividends don't lie."

Here's what they mean: A good accountant can fudge 99% of the figures on a balance sheet or a profit statement. But he can't fake a cash payment. If a company is paying cash, it's hard to fake the numbers.

For example, take Wall Street's favorite number – earnings. Earnings are subject to all sorts of bookkeeping adjustments like depreciation, reserve accounting, and different inventory valuations. Because investors pay attention to earnings more than any other number, it becomes really tempting to manipulate it.

But think about a dividend. A dividend is a fact. When companies pay their dividends, they mail out checks to every shareholder. The money leaves the bank and never comes back. It's that simple.

Regular dividend payments are a real mark of quality. The management and directors know their company better than anyone else. So when a company announces a dividend payout, it's saying, "We have cash we don't need."

A strong dividend payment almost always indicates a healthy business. The company is generating cash and wants to say "thank you" to shareholders. And a company knows if it takes the dividend away suddenly, its stock will drop.

It's not always easy to pay out cash to the shareholders every year... Cash is a scarce resource, and it's critical to every business. So when companies are able to maintain their dividends through bad times, it sends a strong signal to the market that management knows what it's doing... that it has good control of its finances.

Similarly, rising dividends protect stock prices in bear markets. Thus, dividend stocks are by nature "defensive stocks." They protect your capital. A rising dividend acts like a pontoon float and prevents the stock price from falling much.

Finally, a dividend payment signals management's intention to reward investors for offering their capital. As a stock analyst, I place great weight on the dividend payments when I size up a company. A regular and increasing dividend payment is a sign of a healthy business.

Let's look again at Coke. It has paid a dividend for 94 straight years with consecutive increases for the last 52 years. Or take one of my favorite drugmakers, Eli Lilly. It has paid a dividend for 46 straight years.

These types of blue-chip companies carry less than 25% of the risk that the typical risky stock carries. They rarely fall 15% in a hurry, like a "hot" tech stock can.

However, blue-chip stocks aren't exciting enough for most people. Most people would rather gamble on risky technology stocks or something "exciting" like the Facebook initial public offering.

But when it comes to buying companies and socking them away for years, I want big, safe, "bulldozer" like companies that allow me to sleep at night while owning them.

I might not be able to predict which tech company will produce the next hot gadget, but I can safely predict that tomorrow, people will still drink Coke, still buy McDonald's burgers, and still use Johnson & Johnson's Band-Aids. They'll be doing all this 10 years from now.

Below is a list of 12 elite blue-chip stocks that can make up your "shopping list." When the next financial crisis arrives, look to pick these up for bargain prices...

Our Crisis Investing 'Shopping List'

The companies that follow are some of the most powerful businesses on Earth. If you ever have a chance to buy one of these companies in a crisis, the odds are good you will do very well.

You see, the world has a way of not ending... but people still seem to forget this from time to time. And those moments are once- or twice-in-a-lifetime opportunities.

This list is not exhaustive. You can find many other great blue-chip companies in various sectors of the economy. Consider this list a "cheat sheet" for some of the best brands ever.

In the event of a crisis, use this list it to prosper in an emergency.

Remember, an emergency is only an emergency for the unprepared... For the ready, a crisis is an opportunity.

12 Blue Chips You Should Buy in a Crisis

1. **GlaxoSmithKline (NYSE: GSK)** started as a London pharmacy in 1715. It went global in 1830, opening its first U.S. pharmacy in Philadelphia. Today, GSK is a $100 billion global health care company with sales in more than 190 countries. It has nearly 7% of the world's pharmaceutical market.

2. Computing software giant **Microsoft (Nasdaq: MSFT)** operates around the world in many segments of the computing and gaming world. Everyone uses (or at least knows about) Microsoft's software or computing systems. In fiscal 2014, the company sold almost $87 billion in goods and services. It sold $78 billion the year before... Microsoft knows how to make money.

3. **Cisco (Nasdaq: CSCO)** makes the routers and switches that enable information to move along the Internet and airwaves. Its products are everywhere. You can find its equipment in businesses, hotels, and homes. Hilton hotels use Cisco equipment. Starbucks uses Cisco to provide wireless Internet access. The phone on my office desk and the router in my home are Cisco-made.

4. One of my favorite companies in the world is **Johnson & Johnson (NYSE: JNJ)**. A leader in health care, JNJ's diversified business model ensures steady earnings. The company's three divisions include pharmaceutical (37.5% of sales), medical devices and diagnostics (39.6%), and consumer segment (22.9%). The company has more than 250 operating companies globally.

5. **Oracle (Nasdaq: ORCL)** is a $170 billion market cap technology company that provides database services and software to more than 380,000 companies... including all 100 members of the Fortune 100 (the annual listing of the largest American businesses by gross revenue).

6. **Coca-Cola (NYSE: KO)** is one of the world's most recognized brands. Atlanta pharmacist John Pemberton founded Coca-Cola in 1886. Today, it is still creating some of the world's most popular drinks. It's the leader in beverages, offering an incredible array of 3,500 products (including carbonated drinks like Coca-Cola, juices like Minute Maid, and sports drinks like Powerade). Coke sells beverages in more than 200 countries and employs more than 146,200 people worldwide.

7. **McDonald's (NYSE: MCD)** is the world's largest fast-food retailer. Founded by Ray Kroc, McDonald's franchises and owns more than 33,000 restaurants in 119 countries, serving 68 million people per day. Wendy's – the second-largest burger chain in the U.S. and one of McDonald's closest competitors – has only 6,500 franchises worldwide. It's clear that McDonald's completely dominates its market.

8. **ExxonMobil (NYSE: XOM)** is one of the world's leaders in energy exploration and production. It's the largest publicly traded oil and gas company in the world and among the world's most valuable companies with a market cap of more than $400 billion. The modern-day descendent of Standard Oil... Exxon has been minting money for generations and will continue to do so for generations.

9. **Automatic Data Processing (Nasdaq: ADP)** provides business software and services to help administer payroll, tax compliance,

benefits, and health insurance management. It's the dominant payroll services provider. No customer accounts for more than 2% of its revenues, which means it's well-diversified.

10. **Colgate-Palmolive (NYSE: CL)** was originally founded in 1806... William Colgate first started the company in New York City making and selling starches, soaps, and candles. Today, it's a $60 billion world leader in consumer goods. CL's products are divided into four categories – oral care, personal care, pet nutrition, and home care. It sells its products in 223 countries with the help of 38,000 employees. Two of its most well-known products are Colgate toothpaste and Palmolive dish soap. Colgate toothpaste is the No. 1 toothpaste in 146 countries – including the U.S., U.K., and China.

11. **The Walt Disney Company (NYSE: DIS)** first started as The Disney Brothers Studio in 1923. Thirty-two years later, Disney's founder, Walt Disney, opened Disneyland – the company's first theme park – in Anaheim, California. Since then, Disney has become one of the global leaders in entertainment. Disney makes movies, toys, music, video games... It's the majority owner of major television companies like ABC and ESPN... And it has theme parks in California, Florida, France, Japan, and China.

12. **Starbucks (Nasdaq: SBUX)** is the largest coffeehouse chain in the world. It has more than 20,000 locations in 62 different countries. The company was founded in Seattle in 1971. By 1987, it had nine locations. It then was sold to chairman and former employee Howard Shultz, who began the company's rapid expansion. The company now boasts a market cap of $57 billion... and more and more people worldwide keep going back to their favorite coffeehouse on a daily basis.

Crisis Presents Opportunity

Remember... the companies on this list represent the most beautiful beachfront property in the stock market. These are the world's best businesses. They've survived panics, wars, and recessions. They are so good that they often emerge stronger and more profitable after a crisis because their weaker competitors dies off.

But because they are the best, most valuable businesses, they only trade for "fire sale" bargain prices during a crisis... when investors are panicking and dumping all of their holdings.

A rough rule of thumb to remember is that a crisis typically causes elite blue-chip businesses to fall 33%-50%. The next time you see any of these businesses fall that much during a panic, remember that the crisis WILL PASS. And remember that folks will always drink Coca-Cola... They'll always want to take their kids to Disney World... They'll always want a treat at McDonalds... And they'll always use Band-Aids.

If you have my plan in place, you'll fight the urge to flee... and you can step into the market with cash to snap up bargains. You could even make 100%, as investors with a "crisis plan" did with Coca-Cola, or 600%, as some folks did with Starbucks.

The Doctor's Protocol Step No. 4: PROSPER

THE SECRETS OF
SURVIVAL

Congratulations on completing the four steps of my Doctor's Protocol.

1: PREPARE

2: PROVISION

3: PROTECT

4: PROSPER

I hope you implemented all the suggestions I provided. If so, you've built a rock-solid foundation of emergency readiness. I'd like to believe 9/11 hero Rick Rescorla would approve.

Still... our work here is not complete. In conducting my research, I discovered many acute crisis situations where having a little extra knowledge could make the difference between life and death.

These lifesaving techniques and secrets should be taught in every school to every citizen.

But because the government and big corporations treat us like children... because they think we can't handle the truth about risks, crisis, and life-and-death information... few Americas know these things – except for the folks who work in these particular fields.

That's why I've decided to include these extra points here. They will augment what you've already learned. Pay close attention to what you are about to read. These items contain...

The Secrets of Survival

1. Fire. I've explained **fire kills more Americans in a typical year than all other disasters combined.** This is your No. 1 threat to your family's physical wellbeing.

As children, we're taught to "stop, drop, and roll"... but that's where most fire-safety training ends. We're never given more detailed knowledge. Knowing the facts below will increase your chances of surviving a fire.

*** In the U.S., statistics show December and January are the months with the highest number of fire fatalities. Most home fires are caused by cooking equipment. Make sure your smoke detectors are functioning. I check mine on a quarterly basis. Put in earplugs and press the button on the detector until it sounds.

*** Many people make sure their fire extinguishers are charged... but then have no concept of proper use. They aim the flow at the flames themselves. This is a pointless waste of extinguishing agent. Remember, you'll only get about 10 seconds of flow from a fully charged extinguisher.

Aim the flow at the base of the flames. You extinguish the fire by removing or dampening the fuel that is burning. Spray the base in a horizontal sweeping motion.

Remember the acronym P.A.S.S. for effective extinguisher use:

- **P**ull the safety **pin**.
- **A**im the nozzle **at the base** of the flames.
- **S**queeze the handle slowly to discharge the agent.
- **S**weep side to side.

*** In a fire, **smoke inhalation is most likely to kill you**, not the flames. That's why it's vital to have functioning smoke detectors in your home.

If the smoke detectors go off in the middle of the night, **do NOT bolt up out of bed.** This will bring your nose and mouth right into the thick of the smoke. Inhaling will fill your lungs with scalding, toxic smoke.

Practice rolling out of bed when a smoke alarm goes off. Crawl on your hands and knees to escape.

*** On average, you've got about 60 seconds to escape exposure to noxious smoke before dying. You can increase your survivability by donning what is known as a "smoke hood."

It's a device similar to a gas mask. Depending on the model, you can get 15 to 30 minutes of breathable air by wearing a smoke hood. You can get a good quality smoke hood for about $65 on Amazon.

*** If you've donned a smoke hood, do NOT become complacent. You may have 15 to 30 minutes of breathable air, but fires grow exponentially. **A fire doubles in size every 90 seconds.**

Flashover – where flammable gas in a room spontaneously combusts – occurs five to eight minutes after the fire starts. Flashover ignites everything in the room. This environment no longer sustains human life. Get out before Flashover!

*** **Devise a comprehensive fire evacuation plan and practice it.** Make sure everyone knows the routes and the meet-up location. Remember, if you have to stop and think it through, you won't have time to escape.

You can visit your local fire station and ask for assistance in taking all necessary fire precautions.

*** Don't forget about fire safety on vacation... Every time you check into a hotel, **locate the stairs and take them one time.** It's good exercise, and it plants in your mind where to go in an emergency. If the fire alarm goes off, you'll know exactly what to do, without giving it a second thought.

2. Crashes. Stories of horrific plane crashes seize the mind. Many people report dying in a plane crash as their gravest fear. But the statistics don't support their anxiety.

When flying within the U.S., the average person's odds of dying in a plane crash are one in 60 million (yes, 1 in 60,000,000). Put another way... you could fly every day for 164,000 years before dying in a crash. When flying internationally, crash odds increase, but not exponentially. Even when flying on a Third World airline, the odds of crashing are 1 in 2 million.

By comparison, your odds of dying in a car crash are one in 9 million (1 in 9,000,000). That's about seven times greater than the chances of dying in a domestic plane flight.

The facts speak for themselves. The numbers are minuscule. Still, if you ever find yourself in one of these situations, there are steps you can take to improve your chances of survival.

*** Most people are conditioned to think plane crashes kill everyone aboard. They ignore the safety briefings and neglect to read the safety handout. The facts say otherwise. More than 95% of people survive plane crashes... so it is vital you pay attention and prepare yourself ahead of time. It can save your life.

*** In fatal airplane crashes, most people survive the initial impact. It's the subsequent fire and smoke that kills them. Most people think they've got around 30 minutes to evacuate a burning plane. The truth is **you've got about 90 seconds to get out.**

*** The best places to sit on an airplane are within **five rows of an exit.** Beyond this, you have marginally more mobility sitting in an aisle seat instead of the middle or window.

Even if you can't choose a seat within five rows of an exit, the most important thing to do is have a mental escape plan (and a backup) of how to exit the plane in the event of an emergency.

*** Forget about your carry-on items. They will cause delay and clog escape routes.

*** Learn the rule of **Plus Three/Minus Eight.** Airlines teach this to flight attendants. The rule says the most dangerous times of any flight are in the first three minutes after takeoff and the last eight before landing.

Be extra vigilant during these times. So don't get drunk before boarding and don't sleep until you feel the wheels hit the ground. Be prepared to execute your evacuation plan.

*** If the plane loses cabin pressure at altitude, **you've got less than a minute to get your oxygen mask on before passing out.** At that point, you may die from asphyxiation if someone else doesn't get a mask on you. That's why it's imperative to get your own mask on right away. You need to be functioning so that you can help your children and others don their masks.

*** The biggest change survival experts make in their own lives is to cut down on driving. This is especially true during the late night hours, where the odds of encountering drunk drivers rise.

*** The best way to avoid injury in an automobile crash has nothing to do with seat belts or airbags. It is to lose weight. Stay healthy. When in motion, greater mass equals greater force. That also means greater internal damage when brought to a sudden, jolting stop.

Overweight people also have more health problems in general. This makes it harder to fight through serious injury.

There is a huge lesson here. Most people think of the benefits of living a healthy lifestyle in terms of longevity and richness. But maintaining good health will also improve your odds of surviving any number of acute emergencies. It's one of your best overall defenses.

3. Stress. Stress is not something we tend to think of as an acute problem. We think it's something that mounts over time... until it finally ends up causing a nervous breakdown or a heart attack.

The reality is stress poses both an acute and protracted problem. Mental fatigue makes it easier to slip into negative panic in an emergency. Physical fatigue leaves you weak and ineffectual when you need it most in a crisis. And of course, mental and physical strain does mount over time. Stress has terrible effects on overall good health.

Whether you are dealing with an acute or long-term problem, you must know how to handle stress.

*** The best things you can do to prepare your body to handle the stress of any crisis are as follows:

1. Eat well
2. Sleep well
3. Practice meditation
4. Combat Breathing

The easiest way to **eat well** is to avoid what I call the "white killers": sugar, white rice, and white bread. These are high glycemic index foods... and they wreak havoc on your health.

Sleeping well means getting at least seven hours of sleep per night. If you sleep any less, try to take a nap during the day to make up for it.

Lastly, **practicing meditation** can take as little as 10 minutes per day. Meditation is primarily a breathing exercise. You can practice meditative breathing while driving or at your desk. It is one of the best ways to handle stress I've ever come across.

You may recall that our first crisis response should always be "combat breathing." This is where we start breathing in the pattern inhale, pause, exhale, and pause again for four seconds each.

I'll bet most soldiers and cops who do "combat breathing" - the 16 second cycle from earlier in the book - don't realize they're basically practicing "emergency" meditation. Regular meditation provides focus, relaxation, and discipline. It calms the mind and neutralizes stress.

Clinical tests show regular meditators had 5% thicker prefrontal cortex brain tissue than those who don't practice it. The prefrontal cortex regulates emotions, attention, and working memory. All of this helps you control stress and carry out whatever you need to do.

If you've never meditated before, I recommend trying the website www.susanpiver.com. Susan is a Buddhist practitioner who puts out one new, free meditation videos per week. (Her site also includes a large archive of old videos.) You can open one of her free videos and learn to meditate any time that is convenient for you. Just sign-up for her UHP free plan.

Practicing meditation will also allow you to understand the benefits of "combat breathing" the second a crisis hits. This will help you keep your heart rate in the optimal range for survival.

*** In the 1980s, a police instructor began to track correlations between heart rate and successful crisis performance. He discovered people perform best when their heart rates are between 115 and 145 beats per minute (bpm). At this rate, people tend to see clearly, react quickly, and manage complex motor skills well (e.g., driving).

Unfortunately, most people are unprepared for crisis. Their heart rates skyrocket from 75 bpm (typical resting rate) to more than 200 bpm. This makes them unfit to handle much of anything.

Tactical, meditative breathing alone will help keep your heart rate down. Combining this technique with even a rudimentary plan (like taking note of where the exits are before a crisis hits) will keep your heart rate in the optimal range.

*** Tactical breathing calms you in a chaotic environment. It will help you focus and think. But the content of your thoughts is important, too. One thing you must avoid is the "Stockdale Paradox."

The paradox is named after Admiral James Stockdale. He was the highest ranking U.S. prisoner of war in the Vietnam conflict. The condition deals with excessive unrealistic optimism.

In general, optimists tend to survive crises better than other personality types. But excessive, baseless optimism can lead to death. Stockdale describes the paradox best in his own words:

> *You must never confuse faith that you will prevail in the end –*
> *which you can never afford to lose – with discipline to confront the*
> *most brutal facts of your current reality, whatever they might be.*

In other words, convincing yourself that rescue is imminent, only to be let down again and again, breaks the heart and destroys the will to keep fighting. It causes emotional exhaustion. It is often fatal.

*** You should start teaching this "realistic optimism" to your children from a young age so that they will be confident and prepared. It is natural to want to shield your kids from the brutal truths of reality. But this does nothing to help them. Crisis and trauma are things we will all face in our lives.

Don't lie to them and say "Don't worry, bad things will never happen to you." This leaves them unprepared and vulnerable.

Instead say something like, "Bad things do happen sometimes, but you will have the strength and the resources to handle them. We'll prepare together so you will come out OK."

This realistic optimism – backed up by preparation and practice – is the key to building confidence and strength in your children. It's one of the best defenses you can ever teach them.

*** **The best way to survive a heart attack** is never to have one in the first place. As I've said, eating well, sleeping well, and meditating will go a long way towards helping you avoid heart trouble.

There's another powerful tool at your disposal to combat heart disease: aspirin.

Aspirin is originally derived from the bark of the willow tree and has been used for centuries by healers. Aristotle used it as a tea for pain, and others since have applied its magic. Today, it relieves pain, lowers fever, and reduces overall inflammation.

I take one 325 milligram aspirin every week. The chemistry of aspirin affects the body's platelets for about 10 days. Regular aspirin consumption has been proven to reduce the risk of stroke and heart attack if you already have heart disease. There is also a mild benefit for prventing these events plus lower colon cancer risk via primary prevention.

For people older than 50, the benefits of one baby aspirin a day probably outweigh the risks. The main risk of aspirin is gastrointestinal bleeding. I take aspirin with an enteric coating that keeps it from sitting in my stomach as the drug is released. This helps me avoid these minor side effects.

*** **If you believe you are having a heart attack or stroke, take aspirin immediately.** If the pill has an enteric coating, crush it or chew it and ingest the powder. You need to get the beneficial effects of aspirin into your bloodstream as fast as possible.

*** Your last line of defense against dying from a heart attack is using an automated external defibrillator (AED). If you've ever seen a TV medical drama, you'll recognize these devices. They have two pads that send an electric pulse through the victim's body. The shock is often enough to get a stalled heart beating again.

Personal AEDs sell for around $1,000. They may be the best insurance policy out there.

4. Panic. Heart attacks often result from panic attacks. I've talked about "negative panic" throughout my protocol. By now, you're well aware negative panic is far more likely to strike people in crises than conventional panic.

But panic still breaks out in particular situations. It's important to know the three key factors that incite panic. Once you are aware of them, you can usually avoid these situations before getting swept up in them.

*** Decades ago, a Ph.D. candidate named Enrico Quarantelli conducted research on panic conditions. He published his findings in the *American Journal of Sociology* in 1954. For panic to set in, **people must feel**:

- **That they might be trapped (not that they are definitely trapped; acceptance stalls out panic).**

- **Great helplessness.**

- **Profound isolation (as though you are aware of the seriousness of the problem, but no one else is).**

These terms give us some understanding of when panic may begin. The problem is, they are broad ideas... and difficult to isolate in every situation.

That's why I prefer to think of panic as an overreaction. A minor fright may spark a disproportionate response. If this happens in a crowd, the overreaction can be transmitted and magnified. Soon the response is unhinged from the reality of the situation. That is where panic ensues.

*** The responses to panic are the same as to negative panic. Get your breathing under control right away using Combat Breathing. Then, go about executing your escape plan. Observe how others are overreacting first, assess the real situation, then take appropriate action.

5. Crowds. As I noted above, crowds are one of the places panics are more likely to break out. Humans need about one square yard of space around them to maintain control of their physical orientation. Crowds often become much more dense than that. An overreaction in one part of the crowd can start a panicked chain reaction.

*** The No. 1 way people die in crowds is not from getting trampled in a stampede. It's asphyxiation. The compounded force of just five other people around you is enough to squeeze the air out of your lungs and prevent them from filling again.

Humans can pass out after just 30 seconds without air. After about six minutes without oxygen, the brain dies.

If you ever find yourself in a compressed crowd, begin side-stepping towards the edge of the group. Take advantage of the cluster's ebb and flow. In the moments when the crowd works backwards, step sideways towards the outside. And repeat until you're safe.

6. Natural Disasters. There are some common misconceptions about appropriate natural disaster response. The information below will help you know the right way to act, depending on the disaster.

*** **Earthquake:** Conventional wisdom says to stand in a doorframe during an earthquake. But that is only true if the structure you're in is adobe or made from reinforced masonry.

For most people, the safest place during an earthquake is underneath a sturdy table, away from windows. Make sure there are no heavy objects hanging overhead.

*** **Tornado:** Stay in an interior room with no windows on the ground floor. (The basement is even better if you have one.) One of the safest places is an interior bathroom. Use the toilet fixture to brace your body.

*** **Hurricane**: If you are unable to evacuate, close and brace all exterior doors and windows. Then, lie on the floor in an interior room or closet on the lowest floor in your home (ground floor or basement). Brace yourself under a heavy object. Again, the toilet fixture is helpful for this purpose. It is heavy and bolted to the floor.

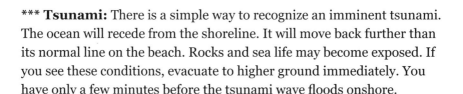

*** Tsunami: There is a simple way to recognize an imminent tsunami. The ocean will recede from the shoreline. It will move back further than its normal line on the beach. Rocks and sea life may become exposed. If you see these conditions, evacuate to higher ground immediately. You have only a few minutes before the tsunami wave floods onshore.

*** Disease Outbreak: Distance yourself from others as much as possible. Do not go to work. Do not go to social events, public gatherings, airports, and other confined spaces.

Protect your orifices (nose, mouth, etc.). Wash your hands several times a day. Use alcohol-based antibacterial hand cleanser if soap and water are not available. And wear a surgical mask if you have to go out.

7. Shooting. The odds of getting caught up in a mass shooting incident are astoundingly low. Despite the recent flurry of high-profile incidents, it's unlikely you will ever need to utilize the following technique.

*** If you are in a public area and someone starts shooting, try to evacuate if at all possible. If you cannot escape, lie down on the floor, face down. **Point your feet in the direction of the shooter.** Turn your head away and cover it with your hands. This will reduce the size of your target profile. It will minimize the likelihood of a bullet hitting any of your vital organs.

8. Government. It's unfortunate, but government responses are unlikely to save you in a crisis. Two days before the 2005 Hurricane Katrina disaster, the mayor of New Orleans delayed the evacuation order. He decided to consult with his lawyers to make sure the city would not get sued by businesses.

Governments also distrust the citizenry finding out the honest facts about the severity of a crisis. They believe it will lead to mass chaos. By patronizing their citizens in this way, they consign many to death.

Do not wait for "official" orders or decrees. **Follow your own disaster preparedness plan.**

Remember, on 9/11, the Port Authority told everyone to remain in the twin towers. But Rick Rescorla instantly implemented Morgan Stanley's evacuation plan. His actions saved thousands of lives.

When it comes to your own disaster response, do what Rick Rescorla did. Take action according to your predesigned and practiced plan.

It will save your life.

Added Bonus: Checklists

All that I have covered in the Protocol is useless if you do not practice it. Book knowledge is useful... but you can never replace practical experience.

You MUST practice your emergency plans on a regular basis.

I prefer to keep current on at least a quarterly basis.The good news is this practice doesn't have to be super time consuming. There is a **great "cheat sheet"** approach to emergency preparedness. It's called using **checklists**.

For example, the military uses written standard operating procedures for every activity it conducts. Checklists are integral to ensuring success. They're an easy way to make sure personnel follow the correct procedures every time. Ask any pilot, and he'll tell you... he won't even think about flying an airplane before completing his pre-flight checklist.

Back in Step No. 1: PREPARE, I asked you to brainstorm your response plans to some of the emergencies you are most likely to encounter. Then over the course of the Doctor's Protocol, you learned detailed steps of how to handle these various crises.

At this point, you can create checklists that codify your response plans. They should be right to the point. Cut out all extraneous data. You don't need explanations in checklists. You just need the appropriate steps to take, listed in the proper order.

Remember, checklists can be physical or mental. Set up physical checklists on paper for your most likely disaster situations. But also make a mental checklist every time you enter a new potential crisis environment.

For example, going to a movie theater and noting where the exits are located is part of forming a mental checklist. Ask yourself, if a disaster like a fire were to break out, what would I do? What would be my primary escape route? What would be my backup route? How would I shepherd my family away?

It's a simple mental exercise of no more than 30 seconds, and it can make all the difference in your survival. If a crisis happens, you will be confident and ready to take action immediately... ready to carry out your mental checklist.

I've included some model checklists to guide your own. Create your own to suit your unique situations.

Then, when the worst comes to pass, you'll be ready and able to take action... regardless of the situation.

Home Fire Checklist

Prior to Event:
- ☐ Complete Doctor's Protocol Steps Nos. 1-4
- ☐ Determine multiple escape routes from home
- ☐ Determine external regrouping location
- ☐ Ensure all family members know routes, locations, procedures
- ☐ Conduct regular fire drills

Crisis Event: Smoke alarm goes off
- ☐ Begin tactical breathing
- ☐ If in bed, roll off and CRAWL out
- ☐ Don smoke hood if available
- ☐ Evacuate just as in drills

Extended Communication Breakdown Among Family Members Checklist

Prior to Event:

☐ Complete Doctor's Protocol Steps Nos. 1-4

☐ Determine what conditions constitute communication breakdown

☐ Establish plan to gather together family members who cannot get around easily on their own (children, elderly parents, etc.)

☐ Determine regrouping location

☐ Establish regrouping time limit

☐ Ensure all family members know conditions and procedures

☐ Conduct regular communication breakdown drills

Crisis Event: Communication breakdown conditions met

☐ Begin tactical breathing

☐ Collect family members requiring pick up

☐ Wait at regrouping location just as in drills

☐ Send out search party *only* after family members have missed regrouping time limits

Evacuation Checklist

Prior to Event:

☐ Complete Doctor's Protocol Steps Nos. 1-4

☐ Determine what conditions warrant evacuation for you

☐ Determine who will pick up children and loved ones

☐ Determine where to evacuate to

☐ Determine evacuation route/vehicle

☐ Arrange for your family to stay indefinitely

☐ Conduct regular evacuation drills

Crisis Event: Evacuation conditions met

☐ Begin tactical breathing

☐ Collect family members

☐ Evacuate just as in drills

Extended Power Outage Checklist

Prior to Event:

☐ Complete Doctor's Protocol Steps Nos. 1-4

☐ Conduct three-day power-free test to determine weaknesses

☐ Secure water, food, and light

☐ Begin six-month rotation of supplies in "FIFO" order

☐ Conduct periodic power outage drills

Crisis Event: Power goes out

☐ Begin tactical breathing

☐ Reestablish power with backup if available

☐ Place blankets on refrigerator if backup unavailable

☐ Retrieve flashlights and other necessities

☐ Live just as in drills

_____**Checklist**

☐ Complete Doctor's Protocol Steps Nos. 1-4

☐ _____

☐ _____

☐ _____

☐ _____

☐ _____

☐ _____

☐ _____

☐ _____

☐ _____

☐ _____

☐ _____

☐ _____

☐ _____

☐ _____

☐ _____

| | Checklist |

☐ Complete Doctor's Protocol Steps Nos. 1-4

☐ _____

☐ _____

☐ _____

☐ _____

☐ _____

☐ _____

☐ _____

☐ _____

☐ _____

☐ _____

☐ _____

☐ _____

☐ _____

☐ _____

☐ _____

☐ _____

_____**Checklist**

☐ Complete Doctor's Protocol Steps Nos. 1-4

☐ _____

☐ _____

☐ _____

☐ _____

☐ _____

☐ _____

☐ _____

☐ _____

☐ _____

☐ _____

☐ _____

☐ _____

☐ _____

☐ _____

☐ _____

☐ _____

_____**Checklist**

☐ Complete Doctor's Protocol Steps Nos. 1-4

☐ _____

☐ _____

☐ _____

☐ _____

☐ _____

☐ _____

☐ _____

☐ _____

☐ _____

☐ _____

☐ _____

☐ _____

☐ _____

☐ _____

☐ _____

More From Dr. Eifrig

High Income Retirement: How to Safely Earn 12% to 20% Income Streams on Your Savings

- $39 -

For the first time ever, Dr. Eifrig reveals his proven options strategy in one easy-to-read manual. This book gives the step-by-step details of the investing strategy he used to close 136 consecutive winning positions... a track record of profitable trading recommendations unmatched in the financial publishing industry.

High Income Retirement contains everything you need to know to begin using this strategy. Doc outlines how stock options work and how to use them to reduce risk. He also debunks the most common misperceptions of stock options and explains why most people misuse them. Finally, he walks readers through exactly how to make his safe, profitable trades.

If you want to trade like the professionals, this book is a must-read.

To order your own copy for $39, call **888-261-2693** and use **reference code BOOKS100**.

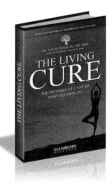

The Living Cure:
The Promise of Cancer Immunotherapy

It's one of the most chilling things a person can hear... "You have cancer." Two in five Americans will receive a cancer diagnosis at some point in their lives.

For the first time in decades, you have a treatment option that doesn't involve removing your cancer by surgery or "blowing it up" with radiation and chemotherapy. You have an option to get better in weeks, rather than years (or worse.)

In *The Living Cure*, Dr. Eifrig discusses...

- A science-backed alternative to chemo and radiation.

- Where to go if you're faced with this horrible disease.

- How to access treatments unavailable to the general public.

- One decision that could double your chance of survival.

- And much more...

Dr. Eifrig is certain this research could save your life or the life of a loved one.

To order your own copy, call **888-261-2693** and use **reference code BOOKS100**.

How to Follow Dr. Eifrig's Latest Research and Ideas

Dr. Eifrig writes three newsletters for Stansberry Research: *Retirement Millionaire, Retirement Trader,* and *Income Intelligence.* These are some of the best and most popular advisories in America...

- Doc gives more than investment advice in **Retirement Millionaire.** He shows subscribers how to invest and collect "free cash" without ever worrying about money again. But each month, he also gives invaluable tips for travel, health, and living a happy life.

For example, Doc has shown *Retirement Millionaire* subscribers how to collect "rent" from investments... two foods that prevent cancer... how to receive a free wine vacation... a simple secret to save up to 90% on local attractions... how to get free golf... and much more.

If you want to know more ways to live a wealthier, healthier retirement, try a risk-free trial subscription to *Retirement Millionaire* for just $39, **call 888-261-2693**

Or you can go directly to our *Retirement Millionaire* order form by typing this unique, safe, and secure website address into your Internet browser: www.sbry.co/0k5cnn.

- In ***Retirement Trader***, Dr. Eifrig teaches subscribers a trading secret that can produce quick gains in a matter of minutes. It's one of the safest – yet misunderstood – strategies in the markets. Yet 99% of investors have never heard about it.

Doc used this strategy to close 136 consecutive winning positions for his subscribers... a track record unparalleled in the financial newsletter industry. Once you see how simple this strategy is, you'll never look at trading the same way again.

Retirement Trader is Dr. Eifrig's most elite service, selling for $3,000 per year. To join this exclusive advisory and learn how to trade like the professionals... **call 888-261-2693**.

- ***Income Intelligence*** has a simple goal: Help readers find the safest, most profitable ways to earn income on their savings. It's a full-service approach to income investing that covers dividend stocks, municipal bonds, MLPs, REITs, and other alternative investments.

Dr. Eifrig uses several proprietary indicators, which help him spot little-known investments that can achieve near double-digit returns with unbelievably low risk.

This service is designed for investors of every level, with simple explanations and investments that are easy to make in any brokerage account.

If you want the opportunity to earn high yields on safe investments and understand all the financial forces affecting your income, try a risk-free trial subscription to *Income Intelligence* for $149, **call 888-261-2693**.

Or you can go directly to our *Income Intelligence* order form by typing this unique, safe, and secure website address into your Internet browser: www.sbry.co/dQl7XC.

More from Stansberry Research

The World's Greatest Investment Ideas

The Stansberry Research Trader's Manual

World Dominating Dividend Growers:
Income Streams That Never Go Down

Secrets of the Natural Resource Market:
How to Set Yourself up for Huge Returns in
Mining, Energy, and Agriculture

The Stansberry Research Guide to Investment Basics

The Stansberry Research Starter's Guide for New Investors